Teaching children with special needs

A Practical Guide for Teaching Assistants

Introduction

This practical book aims to provide really useful information for every teaching assistant (TA) and other support workers in a primary school setting, about a wide variety of special educational needs. Teaching assistants work with pupils with diverse individual physical, emotional or cognitive needs within our inclusive classrooms and therefore there is a need for all TAs to have a broad understanding of special educational needs. It is very much part of a teaching assistant's role to help provide a learning environment which enables every pupil to achieve his potential. Therefore this book has been planned to help all teaching assistants to find information they need about a variety of special educational needs as quickly as possible, and to give them lots of practical ideals about strategies to try with the children in their class.

There are a number of new, exciting and really instructive chapters included in this book, alongside many have already appeared as articles in past editions of the *Special Needs Coordinator's File*. Together they make a book which will provide teaching assistants with ideas and strategies about many areas of special educational needs and how to help children achieve to the best of their ability. All of the 11 chapters have been written by experts or experienced practitioners in a specific field of special educational needs (SEN). Each chapter offers helpful references, web links and/or resources, to enable further information to be gained from other sources if required, as well as clear practical strategies that can be tried in a classroom without further training or expensive resources.

Hopefully this book will provide teaching assistants with very useful basic information about many areas of special educational needs, and enable pupils to feel included in many areas of the curriculum and the social life of the school.

Chapters are not written in any specific order, but the subject matter is clearly indicated by the title of each chapter. There is also a list of abbreviations used in the book and an index.

It has also been decided to use the terms:
- 'pupil' and 'he' for when there is mention of a child
- 'she' for when talking about a teacher/adult in the classroom

for ease and consistency throughout the book.

Finally I hope that this book will be useful to a whole range of practitioners, such as:
- all teaching/learning assistants
- social workers
- carers
- trainee and newly qualified teachers (NQTs)
- police and welfare officers
- home-school workers.

Sue Soan
Editor

Acknowledgements

I would like to take this opportunity to thank all the authors of the chapters for all their hard work and cooperation to enable this book to be written. Their willingness to share their experience and expertise is brilliant and I know will enable so many more pupils have a successful mainstream education. I would also like to thank Frances Peel Yates, Claudia Conway and Miranda Piercy for all of their support and help with this project. Finally, of course, I would like to thank my family, Mark, David and Ashleigh, for their continual patience and encouragement.

Contents

Abbreviations

ADD	Attention deficit disorder		**MLD**	Moderate learning difficulties
ADHD	Attention deficit hyperactivity disorder		**NSE**	National Society for Epilepsy
ADDISS	The National Attention Deficit Disorder Information and Support Services		**OOR**	Objects of reference
			PCI	Positive cognitive intervention
			PD	Physical disabilities
ASD	Autism spectrum disorders		**PECS**	Picture Exchange Communication System
BSL	British Sign Language			
CAMHS	Child and adolescent mental health service		**PEP**	Personal education plan
			PMLD	Profound and multiple learning difficulties
CBG	'Catch them being good'			
CBR	Cluster-based review		**PSHE**	Personal, social and health education
CCD	Central communicative disorders			
CP	Child protection		**PSM**	Physical, sensory and medical
CSW	Communication support worker		**QTVI**	Qualified teacher of the visually impaired
DfES	Department for Education and Skills			
			RNID	Royal National Institute for Deaf People
DCSF	Department for Children, Schools and Families			
			SEBD	Social, emotional and behavioural difficulties
DH	Department of Health			
DIF	District inclusion forum		**SEN**	Special educational needs
EAL	English as an additional language		**SENCO**	Special educational needs coordinator
G&T	Gifted and talented			
HI	Hearing impairment		**SENDA**	SEN Disability Act
HLTA	Higher level teaching assistant		**SLCN**	Speech, language and communication needs
ICT	Information and communication technology			
			SLD	Severe learning difficulties
IEP	Individual education plan		**SpLD**	Specific learning difficulties
LA	Local authority		**TA**	Teaching assistant
LAC	Looked after children		**TLP**	Tactical lesson planning
LSA	Learning support assistant		**ToD**	Teacher of the deaf
			TPS	Think-pair-share

1: Behaviour management
Sarah Whittle

This first chapter of the book will provide teaching assistants with a user-friendly guide to managing behaviour in group situations. Pupils are not naturally inclined to misbehave. Human instinct means that we want to be liked, to be approved of and to fit in. So why do some pupils misbehave, and what can we do to support them?

A group scenario

Imagine the situation. You, as the teaching assistant are taking a reading group of lower-ability Year 6 pupils. On reaching the usual room, you find it occupied, so have to relocate to a small table in the corridor. Everyone in the group seems to be in a volatile frame of mind, ending up with the behaviour described in Figure 1 below. You are also aware that some members of the group are trying to gain the attention of Year 5 pupils in a nearby practical area.

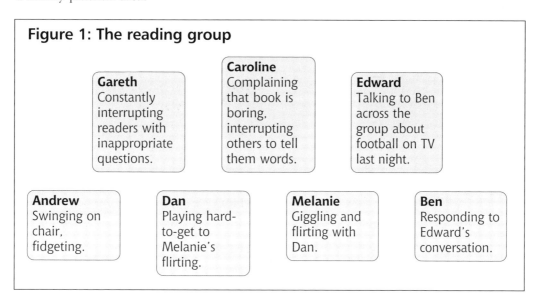

Figure 1: The reading group

Gareth
Constantly interrupting readers with inappropriate questions.

Caroline
Complaining that book is boring, interrupting others to tell them words.

Edward
Talking to Ben across the group about football on TV last night.

Andrew
Swinging on chair, fidgeting.

Dan
Playing hard-to-get to Melanie's flirting.

Melanie
Giggling and flirting with Dan.

Ben
Responding to Edward's conversation.

What lies beneath?

Are these pupils having a bad day, or is there another agenda? Look at the descriptions below of what is going on in each pupil's life, and decide what each of them could be gaining from their behaviour.

Andrew
Andrew had a fight at lunchtime. His mum and dad are having problems. He thinks his mum has a boyfriend. His friend Matt called his mum names, so Andrew hit him. He's feeling guilty, but angry too. He was told off and knows he has to see the head after school.

Ben
Ben thinks that Edward and Dan are cool. Ben likes reading, but he doesn't want to look sad in front of the others by admitting this.

Caroline

Caroline is good at reading, but this isn't consistent. She doesn't find the group text challenging and is annoyed at being in the less able group. This was planned so that she was 'king pin', but she views it as an affront and a sign that the teacher doesn't like her.

Dan

Dan has a hard time at home. He has two elder brothers, neither of whom did well at school, and both were frequently being excluded. They alternately bully or ignore him at home. His mum is supportive, pinning all her hopes on Dan. He is popular at school because he is good at football. Melanie annoys him, but her advances flatter him. He wants to do well in class, but feels that he doesn't need to make much effort in the group.

Edward

Edward finds reading difficult. Because he is regarded as 'cool' by his classmates, he feels he can't afford to be seen to fail, therefore he uses distracting techniques to keep on safe ground (eg talking about football).

Melanie

Melanie has a lot of problems at home. She has low self-esteem and has learned that life tends to be easier if she pleases the males around her. She likes the positive attention this brings. She is quite good at reading, but feels it is not in her best interest to show up the boys.

Gareth

Gareth dreads reading aloud. He's recently been fitted with a brace, which means his speech is slurred and he's inclined to spit. The other boys in the group tease him because of this and also because he doesn't like football.

You have been asked by the class teacher, the deputy head, to hear three other reading groups in the space of an hour. She is very efficient and as you are hoping to do more hours next term you want to impress her. She has no problem with discipline in the classroom. The attitude of the group to you is one of indifference. You feel that, because you are not a teacher, they don't respect your authority. You have tried raising your voice, cajoling, threatening and confronting – with little or no effect.

So what can you do?

Be solution-focused. Look at the suggestions below and see if you can link them to the pupils described above in order to prevent or lessen problems.

Use the language of positive behaviour management

Using the following words should become second nature to you and the pupils you are supporting. Backed up by a clear set of values and a consistent approach they become a powerful tool. Talk with the pupils about:

- rules
- responsibilities
- rights
- routines
- choice
- consequences.

You, as the teaching assistant, are a facilitator who puts the responsibility for learning back with the pupil. You can do this by creating a structure, using rules and routines, which encourages pupils to take responsibility for both their learning and their behaviour. Pupils learn that there are consequences to the choices they make. Pupils have the right to be safe, respected and to receive an education. You have the right to feel safe, respected and valued.

Practise using the language of positive behaviour management in day-to-day situations:
- 'Mohammed, it's your responsibility to clean the paintbrushes.'
- 'Annie, what's our routine for going to the hall?'

Set clear expectations and boundaries

Make your expectations clear at the start of each session and throughout. You can do this by using clear and explicit language, such as:
- this is what we are going to do *(routine)*
- this is what I expect from you *(responsibility)*
- this is how I expect you to do it *(rules)*
- this is what you (and I) will get out of it *(rights)*
- this is what will happen if it goes well and this is what will happen if it doesn't *(choice and consequences)*.

Do not forget that you need to make sure the end of the session is as tight in terms of routine and rules as the beginning. To end a session well is an excellent memory for the pupils and for you!

Distinguish between what is appropriate behaviour in learning situations and what can be appropriate in the playground

Get to know your school's behaviour policy. Clarify your role in relation to rewards and consequences and expect the pupils to do what you say. Use 'thank you' instead of 'please'. ('Just pop this book back on the shelf. Thank you.'). Other strategies you can use are:
- use non-verbal signals where possible (eg hand gestures, facial expressions)
- try 'tactical ignoring' of secondary behaviour – by ignoring smirks, sighs and other secondary behaviours, you don't allow yourself to be distracted and can focus on the behaviour you want to change. Only ignore what you feel comfortable with and what is appropriate to the situation
- make sure you are consistent with other staff by discussing the issue with colleagues
- follow up in private; express disappointment and set out expectations for future behaviour.

Praise

Catch pupils being good and following the rules and routines you have asked for! Look for the positives. Pupils don't value insincere, unmerited praise – the challenge is to find genuine positives. Some pupils respond better to a quiet word in private or a smile or nod of approval within the group. Others appreciate and respond to praise only when it is given in public. This is particularly true for pupils with very low self-esteem and self-worth. Remember, what gains attention continues.

Praise those who are complying: 'Thank you, Dan, you are sitting ready to read. Well done.'

Perhaps the most important aspect of your role is to build appropriate relationships with pupils. Showing an interest in what they do outside lessons makes them more likely to engage with you when you are working together: 'Melanie, you read really well in assembly. That was a lovely poem – did you choose it yourself?' Such comments are important for those pupils who are challenging because:

● they may not experience many positive comments from adults

● it shows that you respect them as people

● other people may hear you saying positive things and do the same

● even if you have to make an effort at first, you may begin to see them in a more positive light.

Relax

Remember that pupils are children and you are the adult. If things go wrong, you need to lay the first plank of any bridges that need building. In other words you need to be the one to think about how to perhaps apologise or say 'I think we started off on the wrong foot today, shall we start afresh?'

Don't be tempted to be over-familiar – it's the quickest way to lose respect. However, do use humour and kindness. Using a calm, quiet voice is really helpful and calming, as is being consistent. We all have bad days, but recognise this in yourself and adapt accordingly – the pupils do!

> When you do need to correct pupils, use the following formula. Tell them:
> ● what you are seeing
> ● how it makes you feel
> ● what you want to see.

Be prepared

● You should always have an alternative plan. Be flexible enough to cope with change.

● Remain calm and humorous, then the chances are that the pupils will, too.

● Make sure that you have enough resources.

● In a heated situation, be prepared to send a pupil on an errand to defuse the tension.

● Familiarise yourself with the task, so that you can extend or simplify it as necessary.

● Be sensitive to what has gone on before the lesson. Get to really know the pupils.

Look for the warning signs of agitation. If necessary, give the group or individuals time to calm down before the lesson proper starts. (For example, Andrew would have benefited from this, giving him a chance to focus and distracting him from his more deep-seated worries.)

Use a positive approach

Use the group dynamics rather than fighting against them. Play to the pupils' strengths.

Thinking about the case studies mentioned above in a similar situation you could:

● use the interest in football shown by some of the boys

● try to engage Caroline by using her as a role model. In private, praise her for knowing so many words. Encourage her to see herself as your helpmate, supporting the others.

It is important to think about finding different 'ways in'

● Get the pupils to express an opinion, and don't be frightened to do the same.

● Use anecdotes and role models.

● Try putting a historical story into a modern context, explaining its cultural value.

● Don't forget to thank them for their contributions.

In any group or class
● 75% of pupils are on your side
● 15% could go either way
● 10% are likely to be the most challenging.

The key is to get the 15% on board. (Research undertaken by Bill Rogers, Australian behaviour specialist.)

Evaluate

As a teaching assistant you need to evaluate constantly 'what went well?' You also need to be prepared to think about the following questions regularly. If you do, your practice will most likely improve and the behaviour of the pupils you work with will most likely improve as well. Using the case studies above as an example think about:

● what could you do differently next time?

● what might you want to follow up?

● why is Edward finding reading difficult? Does he need his eyes testing? Does he have specific learning difficulties?

● is Caroline correctly placed in the group? Does her relationship with the class teacher need work?

● does Gareth need support to cope with his brace?

Asking similar questions of the pupils you work with will most probably mean you will have to seek answers from other teaching assistants and the teachers as well. This is really good practice, because it keeps the pupils' needs at the centre of all planning and teaching. Don't forget that pupils will know whether you are trying to work out a way to work most effectively with them or not!

2: Developing numeracy skills

John Dabell

The National Numeracy Strategy strongly emphasises the importance of including pupils with special needs in the daily maths lesson of their class. This chapter suggests some teaching ideas that you as a teaching assistant can use with numeracy focus groups to support pupils with individual special educational needs.

Learning styles

We all strive to make maths accessible, meaningful and fun, and welcome ideas that make maths a dynamic, exciting subject to teach and learn. Each individual learner has a 'preferred learning style' and these styles are different for every individual pupil, who may prefer just one or a combination of visual (learning by seeing), auditory (learning by hearing) or kinaesthetic (learning by doing) approaches. The most effective ways of learning numeracy concepts are either visual or kinaesthetic – most pupils struggle with learning maths by hearing.

Multiplication – finding a shoe that fits

Pupils tend to use a limited range of strategies when doing calculations. Let's imagine that 10-year-old Helen has only ever been taught one way of multiplying – the standard vertical method, for example:

$$
\begin{array}{r}
76 \\
\times 18 \\
\hline
608 \\
760 \\
\hline
1368 \\
\hline
\end{array}
$$

Helen struggles with this method. She finds it difficult and often 'gets stuck'. This isn't her fault. A dozen examples written on the board don't help either, she just doesn't get it. She always forgets to 'put the nought down' and doesn't understand why she has to anyway – no one has shown her an alternative method of multiplication that suits her style of learning. This shoe doesn't fit, so let's find one that does. Let's try and find a comfortable fit, so that Helen's mathematical experience is one that is comfortable and happy, helping her to regain her confidence. With a little help, Helen can learn a lot.

Visual learning – lattice multiplication

This is a method of multiplication that is easy and fun to do.
Let's try 76 x 8:

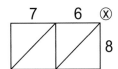

● Draw two boxes alongside each other and divide each box into two cells using a diagonal line. Write the numbers as shown.

● Multiply 6 by 8 and write the product (answer) in the right-hand box using one number per cell. Now multiply 7 by 8 and write the product in the left-hand box, again placing only one number inside each cell.

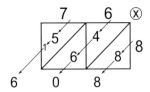

● 'Shoot an arrow' through each cell and 'bring out' the number (draw diagonal arrows). When you shoot the arrows you may have to add two numbers together. For example, add 4 and 6 to make 10. Instead of writing 10 outside the cells, put down the 0 and carry 1 into the next cell (write the 1 in the next cell). Bring out the next number, remembering to add the one you have just carried.

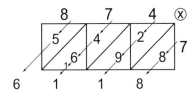 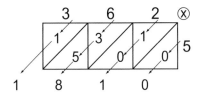

You now have your answer of 608.

As with all methods, practice is the key to see if the shoe fits.
Look at the examples below to see how lattice multiplication works.

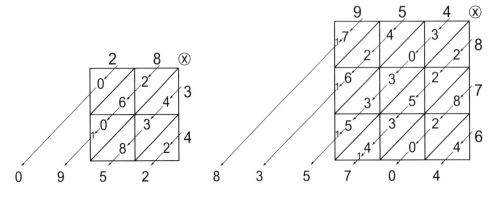

Kinaesthetic learning – multiplication by hand

A highly effective way of teaching multiplication that costs nothing is at our fingertips. Our digital computers are extremely handy tools for multiplication!

A handy way to multiply by 9

● Hold up your hands with fingers outstretched. Let's try 3 x 9.

● Start with your left hand and count along three fingers from the left-hand side (including thumbs). Bend down this third finger.

● Count the number of fingers to the left of your bent finger (two). Each of these fingers counts as 10, so we have a value of 20.

● Then count the remaining fingers to the right of the bent finger. Each of these fingers counts as a unit, so we have a value of 7.

● Add the tens to the units and you have the answer, which is 27. Try this with other multiplications in the nine times table.

● Learning multiplication tables by heart is a major problem for many pupils, but quick access to these facts is necessary for developing maths skills. Learning can be assisted in a number of ways.

A handy way for multiplying from 6 through to 10

● Using both hands again we can also use our fingers to multiply numbers from 6 to 10. Let's do 8 x 9. Start with your palms facing you.

● Each finger is assigned a number. Write the number 10 on your thumb, then 9 on your index finger, 8 on your middle finger, 7 on your 'ring' finger and 6 on your little finger. Do the same on the other hand. Now you are ready to start multiplying.

● Join the '8' finger on the left hand with the '9' finger on the right hand.

● The two fingers that have joined and any other fingers beneath them are worth '10' each. In this case we have seven fingers, so a value of 70.

The fingers above those joined are now multiplied together. So, on your left hand you have two fingers above the join and on your right hand you have one finger above the join making 2 x 1 = 2

● We now add 70 and 2 to make 72.

Try this with other multiplications to test it out.

Finger computation is an art. Some pupils may find that this method helps them get through some sticky situations. Remind pupils that using fingers to do mathematics is perfectly acceptable and doesn't need to be done 'under the table'. (How many times have you done this yourself?)

Visual learning – concept cartoons

Concept cartoons are an extremely effective way of helping pupils get to grips with their mathematics. They present a number of opinions and suggest alternative viewpoints, thereby pulling pupils into the debate, almost as though they are part of the discussion with the cartoon characters. Concept cartoons challenge thinking, spark discussion and promote understanding. They are visual learning contexts at their best – a clear and easy way to get pupils motivated and excited about their mathematics.

Figure 1: Concept cartoon - what shape is the window?

This concept cartoon provides pupils with a variety of viewpoints about a common everyday shape. It can easily be developed into a whole lesson on 'square thinking'.

What to do:
● **Introduction** – give each pupil in the group a copy of the cartoon and ask them to read, together (help them if necessary) or individually, each speech bubble carefully.
● **Individual reflection** – ask each pupil to think about the speech bubbles, then to complete the separate one with a different response. Tell the group that these will be their own opinions.
● **Group discussion** – encourage the group to talk through each of the speech bubbles

together, including their own, to tease out any conflicting thoughts.

- **Share** – ask the individuals in turn to share their thinking.
- **Definitions** – feed pupils word definitions through the course of their discussions to add to their knowledge and understanding. As you do so, pupils may re-evaluate and change their thinking, offering different viewpoints.
- **Investigate** – encourage pupils to explore the properties of the shape.
- **Consensus** – the group discusses further in an attempt to reach an agreement about what the shape is.
- **Plenary** – finish by asking pupils to say how their ideas have changed and what they have learned.

Definitons of words

Use the following definitions to help pupils. As you say them, they can work out whether the shape above satisfies the definition given.

- **Polygon** – a plane shape with straight sides and many angles. It is a closed figure, made by joining line segments, where each line segment intersects exactly two others. Polygon comes from the Greek 'poly' meaning 'many' and 'gon' from 'gonu' meaning knees. So a polygon is a shape with many knees!
- **Quadrilateral** – a four-sided polygon. The sum of the angles of a quadrilateral is 360 degrees.
- **Parallelogram** – a quadrilateral that has pairs of opposite sides equal in length and parallel, and the opposite angles are equal in size. The diagonals bisect each other. Parallelograms have a rotational symmetry order of at least two. (There are some other quadrilaterals that fit the general description of a parallelogram, but which have different symmetry properties.) Rotational symmetry means how many times, as you turn a shape through 360 degrees, it matches the original exactly.
- **Tetragon** – a plane figure of four angles.
- **Rhombus** – a quadrilateral with four sides of equal length. Opposite sides are parallel and opposite angles are equal in size. The angles bisect each other at right-angles. A rhombus has at least two lines of reflective symmetry, and rotational symmetry of order 2. If the interior angles of the rhombus are equal then it is a square.
- **Oblong** – a rectangle which is not a square.

From these definitions we can say that the shape above has six names. It is a polygon, a square, a quadrilateral, a tetragon, a parallelogram and a rhombus. These are best remembered alphabetically as P, P, Q, R, S, T.

Conclusion

The above suggestions are just three ways you can make a big difference to pupils' learning. Talk about these techniques with individual teachers and decide which pupils in the class will most benefit from them. Talk to individual pupils and learn their preferred learning styles. Remember, if pupils can't learn the way we teach, then we must teach the way they learn.

3: Developing literacy skills
Ann Callander

Literacy skills are those skills relating to speaking, listening, reading and writing. Much of the teaching of these skills takes part in literacy lessons, but you may well be asked to support pupils to help them practise these skills and gain confidence in using them across the curriculum.

Practising speaking and listening skills

Pupils need to be given opportunities to:

- share experiences and feelings with others
- interact within group learning situations
- follow and convey information
- respond to books and audio/visual resources
- develop an awareness of audience.

Activities to help pupils share experiences and feelings:

- Ask pupils to talk about a specific emotional experience (eg one that has made them happy, sad, lonely, excited, afraid, worried, angry). This could be related to a story or a poem.
- Share experiences of family events (eg birthdays, outings, visits of relatives).
- Mini circle time – talking about school-related problems and solutions.

Activities to help pupils develop interaction skills:

- **Role play** – pupils can pretend to be characters in a story or people in history, or they can role play particular social situations that help them to learn and understand.
- **Board games** – these involve turn-taking and communicating.
- **Group discussion** – make sure that you allow all pupils in your group time to express their opinions. It is important that everyone feels that their ideas are valid.
- **Reactions** – ask the pupils to choose a reaction, from a choice of two or three, to a particular social situation. Then talk about the possible consequences of each reaction.

Activities to help pupils follow and convey information:

- Taking messages to different parts of the school.
- Following instructions for a game.
- Following a sequence of instructions. These could be spoken or written depending on the ability of the pupils (eg draw round the square shape, cut it out and then fold it in half).
- Pupils making up word trail clues for others to find. This could involve using simple dictionaries to write noun meanings and then placing the word on the object described. The pupils can challenge each other to find the words in the fastest time (eg, It has a flat top and four legs – table).

Activities to help pupils respond to books and audio/visual resources – a few ideas

● Shared reading using big books (predicting events, commenting on characters, recalling main details).

● Sharing interactive stories and non-fiction on the computer.

● Guided reading (predicting events, making deductions, recalling main details, commenting on characters).

● Practical activities linked to story tapes.

Activities to help pupils develop an awareness of audience

● Role play using puppets.

● Reading playscripts with expression relating to the character.

● Giving a short illustrated talk relating to the class topic or project.

Practising reading skills

Pupils need to be actively encouraged and given opportunities to:

● develop visual discrimination skills (be able to recognise similarities and differences between words or letters)

● develop phonic skills (be able to recognise and use sounds within words)

● develop semantic knowledge (be able to understand the meanings of words in different contexts and understand the relationships between words, such as opposites, categories and synonyms)

● develop syntax skills (be able to understand how words are sequenced in a sentence, using the correct grammatical structure).

Activities to help pupils develop visual discrimination skills

● Shapewords – matching high frequency words, as listed in the National Literacy Strategy, to a shape outline.

● Dominoes – matching picture to picture or word to word.

● Words-to-sentence matching activities.

● Spot the difference – searching for visual similarities and differences in words.

● Middle letter change (cat, cot, cut).

● Initial sound change (sent, tent, went).

● Odd word out (hand, land, lend, stand).

● Pelmanism – looking for rhyming word pairs on cards.

● Wordsearches using high-frequency words or rhyming words.

Activities to help pupils develop phonic skills

● I went to the zoo/park/seaside and saw something beginning with... (initial sounds).

● Sound/picture mapping – match picture to sound by drawing lines.

● I spy – initial consonant/vowel blending (something beginning with ca...).

● Missing vowels (b...t) – this helps pupils to become aware that there could be more than one choice of vowels for each word (bat, bet, bit, but).

● Line links – ask the pupils to draw lines to link initial sounds to rhyme endings (b---ed, r---ed, m---an, c---an).

● **Rhyme families** – collect rhyming words ('Can I have a word that rhymes with...?').

● **Blends and ends** – matching initial consonant blends to rhyme endings (bl---ack, tr---ack).

● **Odd word out** – both oral and written (ring, sing, song, thing).

● **Sense or nonsense** – ask children to identify the words that make sense by blending the sounds (brick, quick, stick, smick, trick).

Activities to help pupils develop semantic knowledge

● **Opposites** – using everyday objects (thin/fat pencils, old/new shoes).

● **Sorting** both real and pictorial items into simple given categories (items we can eat, items we use for writing and drawing).

● **Classification** – ask pupils to sort both real and pictorial items into groups, giving their own categories.

● **Odd one out** – ask the pupils to identify the items that should not be in a specific category and give reasons why.

● **Where am I?** – one pupil chooses a place in the classroom to stand or sit and says 'Where am I?' The other pupils have to use a range of prepositions to describe the pupil's position. ('You are in front of the teacher's desk.' 'You are next to the blackboard.')

● **Comparisons** – activities in maths (finding objects that are shorter than..., longer than...).

Activities to help pupils develop syntax skills

● Sort a sentence, using words that the pupils can read. Encourage them to recognise that the word with the capital letter starts the sentence and the word with the full stop ends the sentence.

● Reorganise simple rhebus sentences (words with pictures and symbols). (The software package *Writing with Symbols* could be used for this – see resources at the end of this chapter.)

● Beginning and endings – matching parts of sentences.

● Reorganise subject/verb/object sentences (The boy / was painting / a picture).

● Sentence completion using prepositions – oral and written (The cat was under...).

● Fill in the missing noun, from the choice given. (A ...... was playing football. – bus, boy, boat).

Practising writing skills

Many pupils with learning difficulties find writing difficult as it requires them to use compositional, grammar, handwriting, spelling and presentation skills, all at the same time. Using alternative ways of composing can motivate pupils to write and produce surprising results. They need to be given opportunities to:

● develop compositional writing skills (this involves writing in different ways for different purposes, such as captions, labels, lists, signs, posters, invitations, messages, personal experiences, letters, rhymes, tongue twisters, jokes, recipes, diagrams, maps, stories, poetry, etc)

● develop grammar, presentation, handwriting and spelling skills.

Activities to help pupils develop compositional writing skills

● Draw labelled diagrams related to the information that the pupils have found out about a topic or project.

● Draw comic-strip stories, using speech bubbles for writing simple speech sentences. This can help when introducing use of the question mark.

● Draw a labelled pictorial map or plan to show the sequence of events in a story.

● Design 'Did You Know?' posters. Pupils can present interesting facts, in poster form, about the class topic or project.

● Write syllable poetry. Pupils can start by using only two syllables in each line and progress to experimenting with different syllable patterns. (Example of a two syllable poem – 'Kitten/playing/in the/sunshine/pouncing/on the/shadows.') Counting syllables helps pupils with spelling longer words.

● Use writing frames – these are prepared sheets where the pupils are given a guide for their writing. You can design writing frames for any lesson and make them as attractive as you wish. It is a good idea to make them photocopiable and build up a bank of them for use across the curriculum. (A book review writing frame might have 'The book title was… The author was… This book was about… The most interesting part was… The least interesting part was…')

● Shared writing of tongue twisters can help pupils with sound discrimination and with developing their phonic skills. It can also help them recognise sense and nonsense in sentences. Pupils could compose a tongue twister using the chosen sound. You could write it with their help. Then they could copy the tongue twister and illustrate it (eg 'Six silly sausages sitting on the sand').

Activities to help pupils develop grammar skills

● Sentence completion using simple information. ('A badger lives in a…')

● Now and then (verb tenses, past and present). Ask pupils to choose sentences that can be placed on the 'now' and 'then' boards (eg 'The boy played football in the park.' 'The boy is playing football in the park.').

● Verb change – ask pupils to change the verb in a sentence and talk about how it alters the meaning of the sentence (eg 'The old man limped down the road.' 'The old man ran down the road.').

● Who did that? Ask pupils to match sentences using pronouns as a clue. You can give them a selection of different sentences related to the topic you are supporting (eg 'The postman collected the letters. He put them in his van.').

Activities to help pupils develop presentation and handwriting skills

● Use letter and number templates when designing posters, to help with size and orientation.

● Use word processing and graphics when presenting some written work.

● Practise handwriting joins, in the air, to music.

● Practise handwriting joins linked to rhyme endings in words (eg can, fan, man, pan, ran).

Activities to help pupils develop spelling skills

● **Same/different** – ask all the pupils to listen to two words and then hold up their 'same' or 'different' cards. This game helps pupils to listen carefully to the sounds in the words (eg bat/bag, can/can, band/bend, trick/trick, swim/swing).

● **Rhyme riddles** – ask pupils to listen to a rhyme riddle and then write down the correct spelling on their whiteboards or paper (eg 'I can jump but I cannot jog. I live by water. I am a…').

● **Burst the balloons** – this game is best played in groups of four or eight and is a fun way of checking whether pupils have learned to spell some of the high frequency words. Ask pupils to draw a bunch of six to eight balloons. Then read out appropriate high frequency words. The pupils can rub out one balloon for each word they spell correctly. The winner is the first one to burst all their balloons.

Many of the activities suggested can be used to support the development of children's literacy skills in different areas of the curriculum. You will need to discuss when to use them with the class teacher in order to benefit the pupils you support.

Resources

Writing with Symbols, Widgit Software. Tel: 01223 425558. Website: www.widgit.com

4: Adapting written tasks for pupils with SEN

Anne Callander

As a teaching assistant you may be asked to work with pupils who have a wide range of learning difficulties. You may also have to work in a variety of situations both in and outside the classroom. Most pupils with SEN will need general support with:

- *expressing thoughts and ideas in both group and class discussion*
- *understanding key concept vocabulary*
- *reading for meaning*
- *recording thoughts, ideas and information.*

This chapter will focus on the area of supporting recording pupils' thoughts, ideas and information and it will suggest some strategies that you can use to support pupils with special educational needs in the classroom.

Recording thoughts, ideas and information

There are a number of reasons why pupils may need support with setting thoughts, ideas and information down in writing. They may have difficulties with any of the following:

- **Syntax and grammar** – syntax is about how words are sequenced to convey meaning. Pupils need to understand that the meaning of a sentence changes if words are put into a different order – eg, 'Ben can play football.' 'Can Ben play football?' Grammar is about organising words into sentences, using the correct grammatical word structure. Pupils who have difficulties with grammar tend to muddle verb tenses and their sentences are often immature.
- **Semantic knowledge** – this is the ability to understand the meanings of words in different contexts. Pupils who have difficulties in this area have problems understanding relationships between words such as opposites and word categories.
- **Phonological awareness** – this is the ability to be aware of sounds within words and to be able to use this awareness to read and spell.
- **Visual memory** – this is the ability to recall information that has been presented visually. Pupils with visual memory difficulties have problems learning sight vocabulary or spelling words that cannot be 'sounded out'. They also have difficulty with sequencing activities.
- **Word finding** – this is the ability to recall words from the long-term memory. Some pupils have difficulty in recalling the right word when they need to use it, just as adults do as they get older. Pupils often have to describe the word rather than naming it.
- **Fine motor skills** – this is the ability to use the smaller muscles in the body for precise tasks, such as writing, drawing, sewing or cutting.

A Practical Guide for Teaching Assistants

23

For many pupils with these difficulties, recording information can be daunting. Using alternative methods of recording can make writing tasks not only easier but also more enjoyable.

Alternative methods of recording

There are a number of alternative ways of helping pupils to record their thoughts and ideas. Here are some of them:

- story maps
- comic strips
- charts and tables
- flow charts
- writing frames
- labelled pictures
- posters
- diagrams
- timelines.

Story maps

For some pupils, asking them to write about an experience or event can be quite difficult. They have to remember what happened and then try to retell the events in words. The experience may have been a visit to the seaside or going to a friend's birthday party. They may not be able to recall the events in a particular sequence, but they will want to tell you the whole story as they remember it. If you allow pupils to make picture maps of their experiences they can use the whole page to show where the events took place and may also be able to show a sequence to the events, with prompting.

Labelled pictures

When pupils have difficulties with semantic knowledge and word finding they often need prompts to help them use the correct vocabulary in their writing. Before attempting a writing task, you can help pupils compile a pictorial word bank. It is important that individual pupils choose the pictorial prompts that they feel will help them recall the vocabulary they want to use in their writing. Pictures or symbols can be chosen from a familiar computer program or drawn by the pupils themselves.

Labelled pictures can also be used to support the understanding of a specific area of learning. For instance, you could ask pupils to label parts of the body after a science lesson and then talk about the function of each part. You can adapt the level of knowledge expected to the level of each pupil's understanding.

Comic strips

Pupils who have difficulties with syntax and grammar need support with organising and sequencing sentences, especially when they are asked to recall or compose a story. Using a comic strip format can help pupils organise a sequence of events in a story, using pictures before being asked to write. Initially, you could ask them to write simple sentences in speech bubbles to tell the story or retell an experience. You can use the speech bubble format to introduce the use of question marks and exclamation marks. When pupils are able to write simple sentences confidently, they could be encouraged to write a descriptive sentence under each picture as well.

Posters

Pupils who have difficulty with writing enjoy being able to present information in the form of posters. Posters make colourful displays and the information on them can be shared with the class. Pupils can design a variety of posters relating to information learned in specific subject areas, such as 'Did you know? Discoveries about magnets and materials', 'Fascinating facts about the Romans', 'Amazing animals' or 'Wicked weather'.

You will probably think of many more ideas and so will the pupils. Designing posters is a colourful way of recording information and helps pupils to remember what they have learned. Posters also act as a visual reminder of important facts and ideas, so it is essential that you make sure that these are included on each poster.

Charts and tables

Charts and tables can be a useful way of helping pupils present information. Bar charts can be used to show the results of surveys such as how many pupils have fruit, biscuits, crisps, etc, in their lunchboxes. These charts can then be used as a focus for group and class discussion on the issues raised by the survey.

Tables can be used to classify information. In Table 1, below , the pupils were asked to show how transport could be used for different purposes.

Table 1: How transport is used for different purposes							
My journey	**walk**	**bike**	**car**	**bus**	**train**	**ship**	**plane**
Going to school							
Going to see my gran							
Going to the supermarket							
Going to play with my friend							
Going to the seaside							
Going to Disney World							
Going to the Isle of Wight							
Going on a school trip							

Diagrams

Diagrams can be used to present information discovered during scientific investigations, such as life cycles. They can also be used to present ideas for solutions to a range of problem solving activities. Pupils can show how they solved the problem in the diagram and then use it to help them explain their ideas. Diagrams can be used to show how ideas are linked in a research project. You will need to provide support by suggesting starting points, asking open-ended questions that encourage pupils to think, helping them to find resources, reading difficult information material and helping pupils to develop basic research skills.

Flow charts

Pupils who have difficulty with organising and sequencing their ideas find the structure of a flow chart useful when recording processes like recipes and how to make and do. You can either give pupils a blank flow chart on which they can write, or set up a template on the computer for them to type in the process they need to record, as in this example.

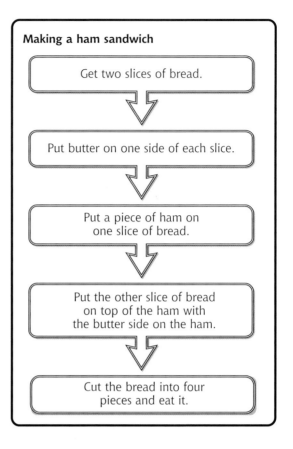

Making a ham sandwich

Get two slices of bread.

Put butter on one side of each slice.

Put a piece of ham on one slice of bread.

Put the other slice of bread on top of the ham with the butter side on the ham.

Cut the bread into four pieces and eat it.

Timelines

Timelines can be used in a number of ways to record information. They can be used to show the events that happen over a period of time:

● to characters in a story

● to historical characters

● to show the timescale of personal events related to individual pupils

● to organise historical events in chronological order.

Timelines can be presented both horizontally and vertically. They can be compiled by both individuals and groups, and can be presented in large format for classroom display as well as small format for individual and group use.

Writing frames

Writing frames help pupils to structure their non-fiction writing and can be used for different purposes, such as:

● to persuade

● to explain

● to describe

● to recount.

Writing frames act as a framework within which pupils can develop their ideas. You will need to help pupils prepare to use a writing frame by talking about the purpose of the activity, the vocabulary to be used in the writing frame and the way it is arranged. You may need to scribe for some pupils when you first begin using writing frames, but gradually they will be able to suggest ways in which writing frames could be adapted to suit their own needs and will finally be able to structure a piece of non-fiction writing independently. The following examples show how book review writing frames can be adapted to suit different purposes.

Using alternative methods of recording can be a way of motivating reluctant writers, especially if some of these presentation formats can be prepared and, if possible, completed on the computer.

The title of my book was:

The author was:

The part of the book I liked best was:

I liked this part best because:

If you are aged ...... you should read this book because:

Title:

Author:

Star rating:

Did you know?

1.

2.

3.

4.

Read this book and you will:

5: Improving behaviour through communication

Melanie Cross

This chapter will help all teaching assistants consider how communication and language difficulties can lead to behaviour problems and provides strategies to help identification and interventions.

The key points to note in this chapter are:
* *Behaviour problems and communication difficulties often happen together. Pupils who have behaviour problems are also very likely to have communication problems. Most importantly, these communication problems may not have been spotted before.*
* *Pupils who have communication problems are at risk of developing behavioural, emotional and social difficulties.*
* *However, there are plenty of simple strategies you can use to make a difference for these pupils.*

Why are communication skills important for 'good' behaviour?

Pupils need good language skills to be successful at school. There is a big difference between the language we use for conversation and the language pupils need to be able to use in school. Outside school the topics of conversation are often predictable (TV, sport, what you did at the weekend) and you can decide what to talk about. In class, the topics are led by the teacher and there is much more listening required. In school, pupils have to be good at using and understanding the following:
* **Complex sentences** – in school, people say things like; 'rule the line before you start' and 'colour all the circles except the little ones'. Pupils are also expected to be able to explain what they have done using these kinds of sentences.
* **Narratives** – pupils have to understand when people explain a series of ideas or the order of events. They also need to be able to express their ideas in order, giving the right amount of key information.
* **Phonological awareness** – in order to learn to read and write and to understand what people say, you need to be able to identify the individual sounds within words, notice the difference between speech sounds and you also need to be able to recognise patterns within words. This is not as easy as it seems, try doing it in a language you don't know.
* **Subject vocabulary** – there are a lot of important new words to learn for each subject.
* **Learning strategies** – pupils don't just learn, they learn how to learn. So they have to be able to understand, remember and use various ways of working with numbers, how to learn spellings, etc.

● **Negotiation skills** – pupils need to be able to use language well if they are to play and work together successfully.

So, pupils who have communication problems can have great difficulty doing what's expected of them in school.

It's less obvious, but no less important, that language is used to think:
● You can problem solve by thinking through possible solutions and their consequences.
● You also form ideas about yourself based on what others say about you.
● And, possibly most importantly, you can think about your emotions and manage them through language. Can you cheer yourself up if you're fed up? Do you promise yourself your favourite things? Can you stop yourself saying what you really want to if you're frustrated? This is emotional management and language plays an important role in it.

Therefore, having good communication skills helps you learn, get on with others, solve problems, understand yourself and manage your emotions; if you can do all that, behaving well is easy!

Why should we try to help pupils with communication problems?

The answer simply is because the effects of communication problems can be long-lasting and devastating.

Communication problems cause anxiety and frustration for the pupils who experience them. Have you ever been in a foreign country, where people didn't understand you and you couldn't understand them? Imagine what it would be like if that happened to you every day and no one 'spoke your language'.

Pupils who have communication problems are very likely to have trouble with learning to read and write because spoken language is the basis on which literacy skills develop, and these skills have to develop before literacy can. Clearly, you need phonological awareness in order to learn to read and write. You also need to be able to understand and remember words (this helps you work out what the word is when you have 'spelt it out'). An understanding of how words go together in sentences and how stories are structured is also needed for understanding what you read, as this helps you predict what's coming next. So pupils with communication difficulties need help to develop their language skills in order to develop literacy. Pupils who have problems with literacy also lose out, because everyone learns new words and grammar through reading.

Learning in general will be tricky if pupils can't understand what to do, can't learn the new topic vocabulary very easily and can't join in with the discussions others are having. Pupils who have trouble talking and understanding language often have great difficulty making friends. They might not be able to say the right thing at the right time or understand subtle but important things such as the rules of conversation. This means they are often seen as a bit 'odd' by their peers and can be, consequently, avoided. Being isolated from one's peers can lower self-esteem and is one of the ways that communication problems can lead on to stress and depression. There is evidence that pupils with communication problems are more likely to be bullied. Also, conflict often arises in the playground if a pupil doesn't know how to ask to join in a game or how to negotiate his role in a game without upsetting others. Pupils learn a lot from each other, so if a pupil can't get on well with other pupils he will miss out on opportunities to improve his communication skills as well as developing his awareness of others.

Emotional literacy is about using what you know about your own and others' feelings to help you decide what to do and how to behave. If you have communication problems this can be difficult, because you need language to talk and think about emotions. Yet another reason why pupils who have communication problems often have trouble dealing with their emotions and with others' emotions in the ways we'd like them to.

It is very important that pupils who have communication problems are recognised, otherwise they will face the problems outlined above as well as being misunderstood. Such pupils are often seen as being uncooperative, when really they don't understand what to do. They may not be able to explain why they did what they did and this can seem sullen. Their clumsy interactions with others may seem to be deliberately aggressive. Then, to make matters worse, adults often try to sort out problems by talking to or sometimes at the pupil and encouraging them to explain things, when it is precisely the lack of these communication skills that caused the problem.

It gets worse. There can be a 'downward spiral' because anxiety and frustration, literacy problems, social interaction difficulties and limited emotional literacy all lead to behavioural problems. So if we don't recognise and help pupils overcome their communication difficulties, their behaviour is likely to get worse.

What can we do?

As communication and social, emotional and behavioural difficulties often occur together, you need to think of ways to overcome them that consider emotions as well as how you communicate. The first and most important step is to:

Look out for and recognise communication problems

If we're going to identify communication problems we need to know what is meant by 'communication skills'. **Think about** what you need to be able to do if you're going to have a conversation (see box overleaf).

Most pupils have no trouble with learning to communicate and they are so good at talking when they start school that you hardly notice any difference between their conversation and that of adults. Nonetheless, everyone continues to learn language and

> ### *In a conversation you have to be able to:*
> ● speak clearly so that people can understand you
> ● order your words into sentences and your sentences into 'stories', so that it makes sense
> ● understand and use all those little word endings; the difference between 'I want sweet' and 'I want sweets' is very important
> ● learn the words you need and remember them at the right time
> ● use all the non-verbal clues you give each other about when it's OK to talk, when you should listen, how people feel, etc.
> ● listen to and understand all of the above when other people use them
> ● use memory skills to help you plan and organise all of this
> ● and you have to do it all at once in a split second.

communication skills throughout their lives. However, there are some pupils who find learning language skills very difficult and these are the ones we need to spot.

It's very important to identify communication problems. Research tells us that pupils who have undetected communication problems might be seen as more difficult than other pupils by both their parents and their teachers. Just the recognition that a pupil is having communication problems changes them (in an adult's eyes) from someone who is being difficult, to someone who is having difficulties learning in their current environment. Often, when adults understand that pupils are not behaving as they would wish because they can't do things, rather than because they won't, tension is reduced. All of us tend to respond well to being seen in a more positive light and taking a positive view of a pupil is likely to help them behave well. So even just the identification of a communication problem can improve behaviour.

Types of communication problems

Some communication problems are easy to spot. For example, pupils whose speech is unintelligible, or who can't use whole sentences as would be expected for their age. However, those who have difficulty expressing their ideas in a logical order in a 'narrative' may not be seen as having problems with language, although language skills are necessary for this.

If pupils don't get on well with their other peers it is obvious, but what might not be so clear is that often this happens because pupils don't have the social communication skills they need. Such pupils often get in trouble with their peers, as well as with adults, because they don't know how to take turns in a conversation, how to stay on topic, how to listen, or how to recognise facial expressions and what they mean. They can make small or large errors, not realising when their friend is upset, or interrupting a teacher, but either way their interactions stand out as odd. This group of pupils are often seen as having 'behaviour problems,' but they may not have learned the skills to interact in the way you'd want them to, so identifying gaps and teaching social communication skills is the way forward for them.

A more tricky group to spot are those pupils who have trouble with vocabulary; they find it hard to learn new words, can't remember the names of things once they have learned them and may say a lot (quite intelligibly) without making much sense. These pupils will find it hard to give precise answers to questions and might say things like 'the Egypt king lived in a funny square thingy, no he died in there!' You can help them remember new words by pointing out what category it belongs to, what letter it starts with, what it rhymes with, what means nearly the same as it does, and by using drama.

Often the most difficult communication problems to identify are the ones that can have the most serious consequences: comprehension difficulties. How do you know if a pupil has not understood what you have said? Unfortunately, pupils who are having problems with language are unlikely to say 'Sorry I didn't understand that, what does … mean?' Indeed the ability and confidence to ask for clarity or a further explanation when something is not understood is often something that pupils with these difficulties have to be taught. Sometimes pupils who don't understand just lose interest (how can you concentrate on something that does not make sense?); they may also copy others or just repeat instructions back. Some pupils have particular difficulty with understanding idiomatic and indirect language, so when someone says 'get a grip' they will hold on to something and if someone says 'don't pull my leg' they may protest their innocence as they are not touching any one's leg, or get upset. So, it can be very difficult to work out whether pupils understand language, but problems in this area are very isolating and the most likely to result in social, emotional and behavioural problems.

A referral for a full speech and language therapy assessment is important if you suspect a pupil has communication problems. A speech and language therapist can confirm the nature and extent of any communication problems and provide therapy, programmes and strategies to help a pupil overcome them. The most effective way to help pupils with communication problems is for school staff and speech and language therapists to collaborate closely.

Then what?

Everyone needs to think about themselves first; it is very important to think about how you communicate and deal with emotions, especially when talking to pupils, as you can be a valuable role model for pupils having difficulty in these areas. It is also possible to make interactions much easier for pupils by simplifying your communication.

Be responsive

Responsive interactions (listening and responding to each other) are important for both language and emotional development. However, it is often difficult to have a responsive interaction with a pupil in school. In class, teachers tend to do most of the talking and often it's not a conversation; pupils are expected to listen and answer questions. The language used is often about giving instructions and information and the topics are limited by the curriculum.

In contrast, in the sorts of interactions which help language develop:

● adults listen as much as they talk

● adults ask pupils what they think as well as telling them things

● often the pupil chooses the topic and the adult joins in

● adults don't tell pupils that their ideas are good or bad, right or wrong.

So, to help a pupil's language develop, you need to listen as much as you talk and try to follow the pupil's lead, without giving your opinion about what they are saying (unless they are suggesting doing something illegal or dangerous!).

Understand the pupil as much as you can

Behaviour is a kind of communication. Often pupils behave in ways you don't like because there is a problem; they may not be able to explain what the problem is, or maybe they don't even understand it themselves. Your job is to try and understand them enough to work out 'what they are trying to say'. Then you can give them the words to say it. Understanding what it's like to be them and how they see things will help you to do this. Understanding why they behave as they do can also make it seem less of a problem. Listening to their point of view and not judging them will help to develop a positive relationship, which is the basis of helping them move forward. This does not mean that you won't explain why some of their behaviours may be unacceptable to others, but if you try to see their point of view, they may be more inclined to listen to yours. An important part of what adults need to explain is where the boundaries are, why they are there and to consistently enforce them, but this won't work unless you consider the pupil's abilities and point of view. It's also important to get to know everyone who lives or works with the pupil; if everyone is trying to help a child learn the same skills, there is a greater chance of success.

Increase self-esteem

Valuing oneself, or self-esteem is a sign of good mental health. How pupils feel about themselves affects the way they act and their ability to learn. Those who have low self-esteem are likely to behave in ways that you may find unacceptable. So raising self-esteem is an important strategy in improving behaviour and enabling pupils to learn. The way you feel about yourself, especially when you are young, is affected by what other people think about you.

So, what you say, do. Even how you look at pupils and your tone of voice can have quite an impact on their self-esteem, either positively or negatively.

Think about: Can you remember something negative someone said about you when you were young? Can you remember something good?

Unfortunately, negative comments seem to be more powerful than positive statements – you remember them for longer and believe them more easily. So, if you want to raise self-esteem you need to think carefully about our interactions with pupils. Those pupils who don't behave as we would like them to get very little praise; perhaps the only attention they get from adults is negative. These pupils can end up not valuing themselves and feeling despondent. If they think you don't like them, because all you do is 'tell them off', are they likely to try to please you by conforming? It's unlikely. However, recognising and commenting on their achievements is likely to lead to positive behaviour. You know about ways to discourage bad behaviour through negative consequences, but encouraging and reinforcing good behaviour can be even more powerful. (See 'Increasing self-esteem', p37.)

Simplify what you say

Something to try: Video or tape record yourself talking to a pupil, or ask a colleague to observe you. How fast did you go? How long were your sentences? Was your vocabulary easy to understand? Did you use any indirect or idiomatic phrase (eg 'get a grip', these phrases 'crop up' a lot)?

You can make the world much more meaningful for pupils who don't understand language well by changing the way you talk. Many pupils who have difficulty learning language have problems with processing speech sounds, even though they can hear well, so a few simple strategies can make a big difference.

If a child has trouble expressing themselves

We are all in situations where we're not very confident about talking sometimes. **Think about** what you want people to do for you in that situation – it's probably the same for pupils, you need to:
● be patient; pupils with communication difficulties may just need extra time to organise what they want to say
● respond to what they say, or the emotions being expressed, not how they said it. In other words, listen rather than correct. However, it is useful for you to give feedback about how they could have said it so that they can learn, so rephrase what they said to include a correct model, eg if they say 'I goed to the zoo' respond with, 'you went to the zoo?' You can also expand what they say slightly to show them how they could use a more complex sentence eg if they say 'she got four'. You could respond with 'yes, she's got four of those blue ones'
● if you can't understand, repeat what you think they said so they can tell you if you're right
● if you really can't understand, you may need to admit it and move on. [NB, stress that you take some (if not all) of the responsibility for not being able to understand.]

Questions can encourage or discourage communication. If you ask, 'What is the name of Henry VIII's first wife?' there is only one answer, and if a pupil doesn't know it they won't join in the discussion. If the question was 'What do you know about Henry VIII or the kings of England?', then more pupils are likely to contribute to the discussion, including those who have trouble with language. Pupils with communication problems are more likely to understand questions about the here and now than anything abstract, so think carefully about which questions you use.

Increasing self-esteem

Praise is crucial

- But you have to mean it! Our body language must say the same thing as the words!

- Establish eye contact before saying anything.

- Building a relationship will help you appreciate each individual's strengths; you need time to observe and appreciate what they can do well.

- Praise specifically, tell them exactly what they have done well. Praise them for effort as much as for what they've achieved.

- Try to identify something special about each individual; 'I've noticed you cut things out very carefully' is much more meaningful than a general 'well done'.

- With pupils who have trouble behaving as others expect, we might have to look hard, but you will find something they do well, so notice and comment on this, even if it's small, eg 'I saw you looking carefully at the teacher'.

- If we want to raise self-esteem there must be about five times as much praise as criticism!

Teach skills

- As soon as a pupil has learned to do something they have a reason to be proud, so teaching, then pointing out what they have achieved is vital. Records and celebrations of achievement are important, too.

- Teach pupils positive self-statements. For example, 'This is hard, but I can do it'.

- Show them, by your example, that if you make a mistake or something goes wrong, you are not a bad person and the world is not about to end. It might even be funny!

- Teach pupils about problem solving so they have ways of overcoming setbacks. You can do this by writing down the problem, thinking of as many solutions as possible and the consequences of each of them, then encouraging them to decide which is the best solution.

- Avoid criticism that takes the form of ridicule or shame because this will only increase inappropriate behaviour and anxiety about learning.

Encourage emotional literacy

Emotional literacy is about understanding your own and others' emotions and being able to talk about them and manage them. It's a good way of thinking about how emotions and communication work together. People who have good emotional literacy are successful academically, at work and in relationships. They tend to be good at the following:

- knowing how they feel

- knowing how others feel and showing empathy

- expressing how they feel

- understanding that emotions are not always expressed accurately

- coping appropriately with emotional situations (being able to think it through, with words, and decide what to do)

- using emotions to assist thought; if you know how people feel, you can work out how they might react.

The best way to help pupils learn these skills is for adults to talk about emotions and encourage discussion about what they might do about them; how they might make

If a child has difficulty understanding language

● Cue them in when instructions are imminent. So make it clear when they should listen. Make sure they know that listening means; being quiet, still and looking at the speaker.

● Gain maximum attention by being at the same physical level, so you may need to get closer or sit down.

● Reduce background noise or choose a quiet environment. Is there anything you can do to improve the acoustics? Being in a smaller group of pupils or in a smaller room might help.

● Speak at a moderate pace; for most of us this means slowing down. This works because it gives pupils more time to process what we have said.

● Insert longer pauses, and more of them, particularly to break up long instructions; again this gives pupils more time to think about what you have said.

● Speak as clearly and carefully as you can.

● Try to reduce the length of your sentences and simplify the grammar. If you make a video of yourself talking to children and try to write out some of the things you said on your video, you'll see how complex adult speech can get.

● Think carefully about the words you use, explaining them if necessary.

● Visual cues often help pupils if words don't make much sense to them. Lots of pupils also find it easier to look and listen. You can use pictures, signs or symbols to support what you're saying, but remember that writing may not help those with communication problems.

● Encourage asking when anyone doesn't understand. Model this yourself and point out and reward others doing it, so that pupils realise it is a 'clever' thing to do. You may need to give examples of the kinds of questions which can be used, eg 'can you say that again please?' or 'what does ... mean?' If adults know that someone has a comprehension problem then they can change what they say in the ways suggested above to make it easier for them to understand.

● Check that pupils have understood, by asking them to rephrase what you have just said.

---

themselves feel better or calm down etc. There are many different ways of doing this. It is also very important to be responsive to pupils' feelings and to recognise that emotions are everywhere!

Tell stories

Stories are an excellent way to learn lots of things about language and emotion. Pupils need to learn the structure of stories, that you always include characters, a setting, at least one problem and its solution. This will help them to structure their ideas when they want to explain or retell events. Pupils can also learn about feelings, including how people 'manage' them through stories. You can also discuss more complex ideas about people's intentions and how you might help other people feel better.

Encourage play

Pupils learn a great deal from their peers, including what to do about their feelings, how to behave and how to communicate. So you need to do all you can to make sure that

---

pupils can engage and play with each other. Some will need help and structure from adults in order to achieve this.

Conclusions

These are the most important things we can do:

● If a pupil has behaviour problems, look out for communication difficulties.

● Think about how we communicate and change it to make it easier for pupils to understand.

● Praise pupils when they are cooperative and behave as we want and whenever else we can.

● Talk about feelings and encourage pupils to think about them too.

6: 'Good sitting'
Sue Soan

For the purposes of this short chapter 'good sitting' does not mean asking the pupils to sit up straight with a finger on their lips, silent and awaiting a further instruction or reward. The importance of correct posture and appropriate furniture is frequently forgotten about in the busy routines of the day. However, if encouraged during the primary school, 'good sitting' can be beneficial not only to the long-term physical health of pupils, but also to their learning. Many handwriting, copying and spelling difficulties can be helped if teaching staff take a look at the physical environment of the pupils.

The classroom

So often our classrooms have tables and chairs that should be the right height for the majority of the pupils within a certain year group, but in reality are either too large or too small for a number of the pupils in the class. Think back to a time when you have been asked to attend a training day and you have been seated on hard, uncomfortable chairs all day. How well can you concentrate on the speaker and focus on the subject in hand? I expect your responses will all have been very similar; that you would find concentrating hard and sitting still even harder! It is no different for pupils, except that they have no option. Pupils need to have chairs that they can sit on with their feet comfortably touching the floor. Tables also need to be at the correct height so that the pupil's arms can rest on the table when he or she is sitting up straight in a chair. For pupils with motor, memory or visual difficulties, a table with a sloping top or a sloping board is extremely beneficial, as will be explained a little further on. Without the correct-sized furniture it is very difficult to encourage good posture and seating positioning to help develop hand-eye coordination and thus good handwriting and word processing skills.

Seating position

The following are very simple rules that as teaching assistants you can monitor and encourage throughout the day for all pupils, but especially for those with fine motor, visual, memory or gross motor needs. Try inventing a song/rhyme to help the children remember what to do.

Seating position
- **Step 1** – ensure that pupils sit with both of their feet flat on the floor.
- **Step 2** – encourage pupils to sit up straight with their backs right at the back of their chairs.
- **Step 3** – model and encourage the children to place their non-writing lower arm and hand horizontally along the desk edge. When they write you will find that their head and arms then form a triangle. This is so important because it both strengthens and supports the spine, and especially the neck. It also provides a good distance between the eyes and the hand while writing (see Figure 1).

If the three steps in the above box are followed it can help prevent the 'slouch' developing (see Figure 2). This occurs when the neck is weakened by inappropriate sitting. Pupils with this problem will use their non-writing hand, with their elbow on the table to hold their head up, while writing or listening. This not only allows the neck muscles to become even weaker, but can have extremely detrimental effects on learning. When in the slouch position, the distance between the eye and the hand is narrowed significantly and the angle of vision is also altered. If this happens handwriting can become inaccurate, and spelling, copying and reading can also be hindered by lack of clear and consistent vision.

Figure 1: Correct posture

Figure 2: Slouching posture

It is also very beneficial if the tables and chairs are arranged for copying, reading and listening activities in such a way that every pupil can look straight at the screen or board. This helps those with memory and copying problems because they then only need to perfect the skill of moving their eyes up and down. If they are positioned at an angle or actually need to turn to and from the board/screen to their paper, the number of hand and eye movements required can actually cause them to forget what they were meant to be writing down and then, worse still, when they turn back to find their place on the board, this can prove to be very difficult.

Left-handed writers

To help prevent spoilt work and arguments with neighbours always remember to position a left-handed writer to the left of a right-handed pupil. Also to enable left-handed writers to sit correctly and to write without a 'hook' position (see Figure 3) always teach them to write with their paper tilted to the right (see Figure 4). If encouraged when young, this will support the left-handed learner in developing spelling and reading, as well as handwriting and copying skills.

Sloping board or tables

If pupils have developed the 'slouch' position or find copying and establishing the right pencil/pen pressure difficult, the use of a sloping board or sloping-topped table is extremely beneficial. A sloping surface actually nearly 'forces' pupils to sit correctly, and also enables them to recognise the pressure that is required to be placed on the pencil/pen to write successfully. It helps pupils with hand-eye coordination problems to copy from the board, and it can even be used as a desk 'boundary' for those who have difficulties sharing their space or equipment (eg pupils on the autism spectrum). Sloping boards can be made or purchased from any school furniture catalogue or even created by using A4 arch files.

A good seating position can be beneficial for all pupils, but especially for those with fine motor and memory or reading and spelling needs. It may be difficult to introduce to begin with, especially if bad habits have already been formed, but persevere and I am sure the benefits will be worth it for both the pupils and the staff.

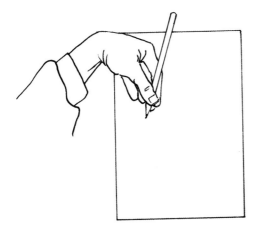

Figure 3: 'Hook' hand-hold

Figure 4: Tilt to support left-handed writers

7: Using ICT effectively in the classroom

Terry Freedman

The basics

As an introduction to this subject let's start by defining a few terms. It's tempting to think about ICT in a very narrow way, meaning being able to type or use a painting programme. In this regard, the Americans have probably got it right, because they call it 'educational technology' which, if you think about it, means technology used for educational purposes. True, it doesn't quite convey the idea of communicating, the all-important 'C' part of 'ICT', but what it does do is open one's mind to other possibilities.

Thus digital audio recorders, digital video, digital cameras – all these types of item can be used to further pupils' ICT skills and to enhance their learning in other areas of the curriculum. Of course, the devices mentioned do not actually have to be digital – but you can do a lot more, and more easily, if they are.

And don't forget that you don't have to restrict yourself to devices as such. The use of the internet, for both research and for communicating with others, is a case in point. Email can be a great tool for sharing views, as can a forum or, if your school allows it, instant messaging.

The term 'special educational needs' (SEN) also covers a wide range of possibilities. At one extreme, it can mean mild learning or behavioural difficulties, and at the other very restricted physical capabilities, requiring specialist equipment. And really, although it is customary to think of SEN in terms of (potential) underachievement, we need to acknowledge that pupils who have been identified as being gifted or talented also have special needs. Indeed, pupils whose first language is not English may do, and taking this further, using the Every Child Matters and personalisation criteria, each pupil is unique and has, in that sense, special needs.

Given limited resources, though, not least of the teaching assistant's time, priorities have to be drawn up. In the remainder of this chapter I will consider how the most effective use can be made of the teaching assistant's time, both in the classroom, and outside it. And it all starts with planning.

Failing to plan means planning to fail

In many schools I've seen, where inclusion is not much more than a section in a policy document, the root cause is not ineffective teaching assistants, but poor deployment of them. Ideally, teaching assistants should be used at all stages of the teaching process.

First, take the curriculum. By and large it is better to start with a curriculum for all. In other words, except in very special circumstances the curriculum should be the same for all pupils (or at least start out that way).

For example, suppose you are in a school that follows the National Curriculum. It is not sensible to have most pupils following the National Curriculum, and some pupils following something completely different on the grounds that they couldn't cope with the mainstream curriculum, according to somebody's opinion. Looked at from one point of view, that approach is prejudicial and even insulting.

A better approach is to take the curriculum and then identify how it can be made accessible to pupils with different types of special educational need. If the curriculum is suitable for all pupils, then we can move on to the level of the individual units. If it is not, then an alternative curriculum should be found, or created. However, this does not mean abandoning the ultimate learning objectives of the original curriculum.

For example, one of the aims of ICT curriculum might be to enable pupils to be digitally literate, meaning being able to recognise when data, eg from a search result on the internet, may be suspect. So any new curriculum might still have that as an ultimate goal. The important thing is to find or devise a curriculum that enables the pupils to reach their full potential, whatever that happens to be, and not to provide a simplified course as such.

A key role for the teaching assistant is to identify the key goals of the curriculum, which ought to be listed anyway, and use them as the basis for an alternative curriculum, or a simplified version of the curriculum that still is balanced. (As opposed to the sort of simplified curriculum that addresses a very narrow range of skills and has a very limited range of associated learning and teaching activities as a result.)

The (perceived) difficulty may lie in the actual learning objectives involved, but in general it is far more likely to be a matter of identifying suitable resources.

This is where the teaching assistant comes into her own. First, she should ensure that she understands what the learning objectives are, and how the recommended resources (if there are any) relate to them. Next, it will be a matter of finding alternative resources.

This is often more time-consuming than difficult. There are lots of resources, but first you have to find them, and then you have to evaluate them. Let's look in closer detail at this.

Types of resource
The kinds of learning resources that you can investigate are as follows:
- printed resources
- interactive websites
- software programs

- reference materials (eg CD-Roms)
- podcasts (digital downloadable audio files)
- video podcasts (similar to podcasts, but video)
- enhanced podcasts (audio podcasts accompanied by pictures that change at certain points during playback).

(At the end of this chapter there is a list of where you might look for some of these resources.)

Evaluating resources

You don't have to be a computer expert to effectively evaluate digital resources. Here is a handy guide to doing so. Teaching assistants should be given time to evaluate resources thoroughly.

What you need to look for will obviously differ according to what type of resource you're considering, but there are some generic criteria. Here are some ideas to get you started:

Will the pupils be able to understand it?

You know your pupils better than the supplier, so put yourself in their shoes. Ideally, a resource should be accessible by a range of abilities. Think about the literacy aspect as well: sometimes a resource would be fine if it wasn't for the level of literacy required to use it fully. This is often a problem with software applications, either because they try to cram too much on a 'page' or because the on-screen instructions appear to have been translated from Japanese to American English by a specialist in French!

What is the layout like? Is it confusing?

This is similar to the preceding point in some respects. There seems to be a common view these days that pupils like 'busy' layouts – but being able to cope with them and actually finding them easy and useful are two different things. Resources should be so simple to use that it's almost intuitive to do so.

Is it accurate?

This shouldn't even need to be a consideration, but let's face it: software writers and authors of printed materials are only human, and they make mistakes. Choose an area where common errors are found, and see how it's treated.

Does it meet National Curriculum requirements?

It doesn't necessarily matter if the answer is 'no', of course, but here is another area where you have to be vigilant – especially if the item is some years old, or from another country.

Is it interesting?

Or, more accurately, will your pupils find it interesting? This is linked, of course, to the following point.

Is it challenging?

A good criterion to use is the Ofsted one: if the pupils can answer harder questions than they are actually being asked, or can do tougher tasks than are being set by the resource, then by definition they are not being challenged.

Are the tasks realistic for the pupils in your class?

This relates to the content rather than the skills (which we've considered earlier). For example, if the resource centres on a subject area which is completely outside the experience of your pupils, perhaps it's not a good idea to use it. For example, a modelling programme which was about running a farm might not be useful in a school where many of the pupils had never been to the countryside.

If it's software, does it have non-computer-based exercises?

It's always good to have a plan B in case the computers can't be used for some reason. Also, not everything needs to be done on a computer, and a good resource will provide a wide range of activities, including computer-based, written and oral, for both individual and group work.

Is it good value for money?

It may be cheaper in the long run to buy sets of photocopiable resources than sets of textbooks, for instance.

Other criteria

There are other criteria which apply especially to software, such as:

● Is the on-screen help good? This means: will pupils be able to easily find answers to their questions – and will they be able to understand the answers?

● Do the graphics enhance the programme, or distract one's attention?

● Is the colour scheme too dull, too garish? Is it suitable for sight-impaired pupils?

● Is it compatible with the school's computer system? You may need to ask for clarification about this, but it's best to buy products which specifically state that they are compatible with the school's system, especially if you have a network. Installing programs on a network is often not as straightforward as doing so on an ordinary computer, as you have probably discovered. For example, the program may need to be placed in a different area of the computer system, and this could lead to some programs not working properly. In some cases it could even lead to people being able to accidentally delete essential system files!

● Is it cost-effective? Is there a cheaper alternative? In software, as in so many other areas of life, the 80:20 rule tends to apply, whereby 80% of people use just 20% of the features of a program. As an example, you may think that it would be wonderful for the pupils, or possibly the older pupils, to be able to use Photoshop for their graphics work. However, Photoshop costs nearly £400 per licence, whereas Photoshop Elements costs about £60 – and there are even cheaper alternatives. Another consideration is whether a site licence is available.

● When it comes to podcasts and video podcasts, these are quite new types of resource, and often produced by amateurs. So, you have to be very careful. Things to consider include:

* Quality of the sound and graphics. Some of them sound like they were recorded with the person's head in a bucket. Making it louder will just make it worse.

* Is it accurate? If it has been made by an expert, that's fine. But if it's been made by someone who is not a teacher or similar, it is probably best to leave it. Assuming, of course, that it's an instructional resource. If it's just meant for fun or to give you access to something that you would otherwise be unlikely to come across, that's a different matter.

* Is it suitable in terms of content? Usually, a podcast or video podcast will indicate, next to its name or description, whether it features 'explicit' content: meaning nudity, violence or swearing.

Hardware

If you are looking at hardware, such as digital cameras, there are other things to take into account, such as:

Is it easy for non-experts to use?

This is probably another area where the 80:20 rule applies. You can buy a digital camera for several thousand pounds that will do just about everything but make the tea, or one for about 30 quid that is nice and simple to use and which gives pictures of a decent enough quality to put in a PowerPoint presentation or publish on the school's website. Your choice!

Is it robust?

It's cheaper in the long run to buy something that's been built with classrooms in mind than something that's been designed for use in a much more sedate environment!

Is it cheap and easy to maintain?

I worked in a school once where the main printer was so expensive you had to call an engineer out to change the toner cartridge! This is not helpful at all: given that things are going to get knocked about in a school setting, you need equipment that is either easy to fix or cheap to repair or replace.

Is it recommended in (educational) magazine reviews?

To be honest, you have to be a bit wary of magazine reviews. Obviously, a good review is better than a poor one, but testing something for a day or two in the comfort of your own home is a little different from seeing how it fares over a term in a classroom of 30 pupils.

Is it compatible with existing systems?

Most things are compatible with other things these days, but you still need to be careful. For example, an Apple laptop may not work with anything else in the school if your school uses PCs. You'll need to check, also, whether you can buy hardware – it may be that the school has a central budget for this, and that you have to make a case for buying anything out of the ordinary.

How new is the technology it uses?

Newer may not mean better, and this applies to software, too. As a general rule, it's wise to not buy first generation products: let others be the guinea pigs, not your pupils!

Before going into the classroom

To be most effective in the classroom, the teaching assistant should:

- understand the learning objectives of the lesson
- understand how the ICT can help to achieve those learning objectives
- be familiar with the hardware and software involved
- be familiar with the individual pupil's needs. These may (should) be listed, whether on the school's managed information service (MIS) or in the pupil's individual education plans, or both
- have access to the school's MIS system and be familiar with how to use it.

Clearly, the teaching assistant needs to be involved in all stages of planning, and given the opportunity to have appropriate training.

In the classroom

The teaching assistant given the job of supporting pupils with special educational needs should:

- set up specialist equipment if any is needed, before the pupils enter the classroom
- focus only on the pupils with special educational needs
- not do the pupils' work for them
- help pupils, where appropriate, by adjusting the computer environment. For example, use the display options (if you have access to them) to make the contrast better on the screen, or use the accessibility features if you are using Windows (look in the Programs-Accessories menu)
- have a range of options handy. For example, if a pupil finds it hard to manipulate the mouse, try a tracker ball instead.

Useful resources

The Teacher Resource Exchange features a wide range of resources created by other teachers. Some are finished products, while others are half-formed ideas that may give you ideas. They are not officially recommended, as the government doesn't undertake any quality assurance of the materials. http://tre.ngfl.gov.uk

The inclusion website has ideas, means of communicating with others, and resources. http://inclusion.ngfl.gov.uk

You can find a variety of videos and podcasts on the internet. For example, look at www.film.com/tv.

If YouTube is banned in your school, try TeacherTube instead. It has a growing number of videos which are, as the name implies, made for or by teachers (www.teachertube.com).

For podcasts, look in iTunes (www.apple.com/itunes) and go to the Store, where you can preview podcasts and video podcasts, download them, and subscribe to them. For a specifically educational resource, you could do a lot worse than go here: http://epnweb.org. The one drawback is that it is primarily American.

Useful websites include the following

A good range of products may be found here, for a range of special educational needs: www.inclusive.co.uk

The Ace Centre, based in Oxford, also has a range of information on its website: www.ace-centre.org.uk

The www.senict.co.uk/sitemap.htm website has some useful examples of ICT being used to support children with SEN, although it is not the most interesting site I've come across.

Becta has a very good range of documents on the subject of SEN and ICT, although some of the terminology used appears somewhat dated. The easiest way to find it is to go to http://schools.becta.org.uk and then use the site's search facility to look for ICT and SEN. Then click on the link about planning for inclusion.

See www.ictineducation.org for further details about the author and other articles.

There are also some specialist websites, such as:
● The British Dyslexia Association www.bdadyslexia.org.uk
● The Royal National Institute for the Deaf www.rnid.org.uk/information_resources
● The Royal National Institute for the Blind www.rnib.org.uk
● The Dyspraxia Association www.dyspraxiafoundation.org.uk

Conclusion

Using ICT effectively in the classroom for pupils with special educational needs requires a commitment from the school that goes beyond allocating a teaching assistant to a class, or even an individual pupil. It involves planning at several levels, and the provision of an effective continuing professional development (CPD) programme. And it involves finding, and then carefully evaluating, resources for use in the classroom.

8: Spelling tips
Hilary Broomfield

This chapter will discuss how pupils learn to spell in a classroom and how you, as teaching assistants, can help them develop their skills and abilities.

Classroom support for spelling takes different forms:
- teaching letter sounds
- helping pupils learn spellings
- setting spelling lists
- testing spellings
- supporting spelling in everyday writing.

Learning to spell and learning styles

Whichever activity you are involved in, it is important to recognise that individual pupils will approach tasks in different ways – this is usually referred to as 'learning style'. For example:

Visual learners

Visual learners (V) tend to prefer learning spellings through looking at words and letter shapes (graphemes), spotting common patterns and letter strings. When trying to recall a word, they 'see' it in their mind's eye and tend to say 'Does this look right?' They may write several variations of a word and compare them before selecting the one they are happy with. They also use letter names rather than sounds when talking about a word.

Auditory learners

Auditory learners (A) prefer listening to words, 'tuning in' to syllables and letter sounds (phonemes) and 'sounding these out' in a sequence. As they write them down, they say the word syllable by syllable, or sound by sound, checking and listening to hear if it is right. They tend to use letter sounds and/or names.

Kinaesthetic learners

Kinaesthetic learners (K) like 'hands-on' practical tasks; they learn a word through writing it down and 'feeling' the movement and shape. They may write a word several times and use this alongside looking at the word to get a sense of whether it 'feels' and 'looks' right.

Of course, many learners are a mix of the above. Competent adult spellers tend to use visual memory to recall words, only returning to auditory techniques as back-up for new words or longer 'tricky' ones.

The current emphasis on synthetic phonics will benefit many pupils, but it must be remembered that some pupils may have auditory processing difficulties and may respond better when there is visual and kinaesthetic support. Having a 'support kit' of techniques and resources that offers a choice or combination of learning methods provides a 'multi-sensory approach', which benefits all learners. This is also referred to as 'VAKing'. It prevents problems arising from adopting just one method, where the pupil's style is at odds with the teaching assistant's or the teacher's.

Visit the website www.standards.dfes.gov.uk/local/clld/las.html to see the government scheme 'Letters and Sounds' for word and sentence lists to use with the various techniques described here.

Multisensory support

This encourages the learner to use their strengths alongside other techniques, through:
- looking carefully at letter shapes and patterns
- saying letter sounds and words and feeling the 'sound shape' in the mouth as it is spoken
- hearing letter sounds and their 'sound position' within words – beginning, middle or end?
- writing or moving letters shapes into position – feeling the shape and sequence of letter patterns and words.

Teaching new letter sounds

If you are new to this, you may need to check the following:
- Do you say sounds 'purely'? Without an 'er' sound at the end, eg try not to say 'ber' for 'b'. This helps pupils both when they need to blend sounds together for reading and when they try to break words down for spelling.
- How to write the letter in the correct way. Which form is required – printed, joined, upper or lower case?
- The examples of words you are going to use follow the pattern you are trying to teach. Do not use irregular words or words that contain a different pattern or sound, eg for the short vowel sound /e/ use words such as 'egg,' 'pen,' 'elf'. Do not use words such as 'said', 'head' or 'equal'.
- You use the terms 'letter name' or 'grapheme' when you are referring to the alphabet name of the letter, eg 'bee' and the terms 'sound' or 'phoneme' when referring to the 'sound' that letter makes in a word eg /b/
- That you introduce letter sounds in a systematic way, either though the scheme in use in your classroom or through the government one – 'Letters and Sounds'.

For each new letter sound, carry out the following activities with the pupils.

Listen and say
- **Listen** to a word that contains the target sound.
- **Say** the whole word together.
- **Say** the sound (phoneme) you are listening for.

- **Ask** where the sound occurs in the word – beginning, middle or end?
- Encourage the pupils to **say** other words that have the same sound.
- **Talk** about the position of the phoneme in the word.
- **Say** the word within a sentence so that it is understood.

Look and say

- **Look** at the letter shape/s (grapheme) representing the sound.
- **Look** at the word or letter pattern containing the grapheme from left to right.
- **Name** the letters.
- **Examine** the grapheme in its different forms – lower case, upper case and handwritten.
- **Link** it to the phoneme; you can also link it to a picture clue, eg 'b' for 'ball'.

Look and move

- **Find** plastic letter shapes/letter cards to **match** the grapheme.
- **Move** the letter shapes into a left to right order to **make** the pattern/word.
- **Name** the letters and say their **sounds** as you **make** the word.

Write and say

- Teach the pupils how to **write** the letter.
- **Feel** the shape by drawing it large in the air and **talk about how to form** it – use a commentary – 'all the way round, up and down'.
- **Name** the letter and say its **sound** it as you write.
- **Place** it in its correct position on a line.
- **Size it** – how high is it compared to other letters?
- **Practise** how to join it to other letters.

Use it

- **Use** the new letter alongside letters that are already known.
- **Look at and learn** more words with the same pattern.
- **Include** the sound in listening games.
- **Blend** the new sound/pattern with other letter sounds to make new words.
- **Break down (segment)** whole words that contain this sound into its individual letter sounds.
- **Use** the letter sound pattern in sentence dictation.
- **Look** for it and **highlight** it in reading activities.

Learning spellings

Learning spellings is more than being given a list to take away and remember. It is important to:

- introduce new words first and talk about them, in this way they are made more memorable
- show pupils ways to learn words – don't just leave them to it!
- encourage pupils to use methods that suit them.

Introducing a new word or group of words of the same pattern
Choose one word or a small group of up to four words

Before you begin…
Ask yourself:

- if the words are phonically regular or irregular
- if they are regular – has the pupil covered all the letter patterns within the word yet?
- if the answer is yes, then use letter sounds and names and a full multisensory approach (see below)
- if the word is irregular or contains letter sound patterns not yet covered, then use only the visual and kinaesthetic techniques described here – explain that this word is to be learned in a different way and do not refer to the sounds.

Introducing new words in a multisensory way

- Write each word on a whiteboard pausing between each letter.
- **Name** the letters.
- If there is a regular sound pattern, say the individual sounds, if not, don't.
- Talk about the meaning of the words.
- **Say some sentences** with them in.
- For each word, ask 'Have you seen this word somewhere before? Where?'
- Rub out each word, then present it again, one letter at a time, as before.
- Examine the word carefully. What letter/sound does it **begin** with? What is in the **middle**? What is at the **end**?
- **Ask questions** about the letters/sounds in the words (see below).
- **Highlight any interesting parts** of the word you have discovered.
- **Sky write** the word in the air together as you name the letters (and sounds if appropriate) one by one again.
- **Make it** with plastic letters/letter cards, always moving from **left to right** and talking about the interesting points you have discovered.
- **Write it** together on mini-whiteboards.
- **Scan for it** and find it somewhere else, eg a dictionary, on a lotto board, in a text.
- Do the same for the other words in the group, talking about their similarities and differences.

Questions to ask when looking at words
The following are questions you can ask yourself first and then ask the pupils:

- Which letter comes **before/after** another… eg which letter comes before the 'e' after the 't'?
- Is the word **long or short**?
- **How many letters** does it have?
- How many **consonants**? How many **vowels**?
- Are there any **double or repeated** letters?
- Does it **begin and end** with the same letter?
- Does it remind you of a word you already know? Which one and why?

- What is the **same and different** about them?
- Does it share the **same pattern or rime** as a word you already know?
- Are there any **hidden words** within the word, eg the 'is' in 'this'?
- Does it have a **suffix or a prefix**? (older/ more able pupils only)
- Is there anything '**odd**' about the word, eg a silent letter?

How to learn words

Talk to pupils about **how to learn** new words. What do they usually do? Which way is the most effective for them? Encourage a '**little and often**' learning routine rather than trying to learn something in one long session.

Demonstrate other things pupils can do to learn words that they might not have thought of (see below). Ask them to try them and see if they are helpful. Think about how these link with the learning styles mentioned at the beginning.

One of the most common ways to learn spellings is '**Look, Cover, Write, Check**'. Saying and naming the letters is added in here too. 'Sounding out' the letters can be added if the word is regular.

1. **Look** carefully at the word
2. Say the word
3. Name the letters
4. **Cover** up the word
5. **Write** the word saying the letters again as you write
6. **Check** the word – were you right?
7. Practise it again!

Longer and trickier words may need some extra help and this method will not work for everyone.

Break words into their patterns
- Use space to separate the sec-tion-s.
- Use colour to highlight patterns.
- Draw a box or circle round the tricky bits to remember.
- Find similar patterns in words and learn them as a set – station, explanation, nation.

Use mnemonics
Mnemonics are memory devices to help remember tricky words, for example, saying a sentence where the first letter of every word spells out a target word, eg: Big Elephants Can Always Understand Small Elephants (BECAUSE).

'Deconstruct' words
- Break longer words down into blocks.
- Learn the different blocks.
- Use these to complete the partial word several times.

- Take out more and more letters from each block each time:
  - ❊ beautiful
  - ❊ beau-ti-ful
  - ❊ beau-ti f_ _
  - ❊ beaut- ti _ _ _

Look for words within words

- 'Here' is in the word 'there'.
- 'Man' is in the word 'woman'.

Play with the tricky bits

Find the tricky bits/interesting patterns and:

- colour these
- make them larger
- use different fonts
- cut them up
- move them around
- put the words on an interesting background
- play with them on an interactive whiteboard.

As you visualise these words and talk about them, give them sound effects, write them in the air – make them memorable!

Missing letters

'Missing letters' is useful for small groups and individuals. Use letter names if working visually, or with irregular words. Use sounds if working with regular words or backing up auditory work you have carried out.

Start this strategy off by presenting the target word one letter at a time from left to right. Then:

- name the letters
- pupils repeat
- pupils look away
- teacher covers/erases first letter of the word
- pupils look back
- pupils name the missing letter
- replace the letter in the word
- repeat with the second letter of the word
- repeat with the third letter, etc, working through the word from left to right
- now cover letters out of sequence
- gradually make the task harder covering two letters, three letters at a time.

A further technique that some older pupils may benefit from is the neuro linguistic programming (NLP) spelling routine. It is particularly useful for those who prefer a visual approach.

NLP word learning

- Place the word in front of you.
- Think something pleasurable/funny/interesting about it.
- Look up left and visualise the word – seeing it in your 'mind's eye'
- Write the visualised word.
- Check it and correct it if you need to.
- If you had to correct it, look up left again and visualise the correct word.
- Write it again.
- Check it again.
- Do this until you are writing it correctly.

NLP word recall

- When you need the word later, think the thought you had about the word.
- Look up left to visualise the word
- Write it.

Setting spellings

Sometimes teaching assistants may be asked to create a spelling list for a group or individual. It is important to give the list careful thought. The teaching assistant's knowledge of the teaching that individuals and groups have already received is important here; wherever possible, link to this. Introduce the words in the way already described, and then pupils are only asked to work on words they are familiar with and that are within their grasp.

Which words?

Link the words in spelling lists to at least one of the following:

- assessments/IEPs (individual education plan)
- current letter sounds and words covered in classroom/support lessons
- any phonic/reading schemes that are being followed
- a pupil's personal interests
- National Literacy Strategy high and medium frequency words
- words you have noticed causing problems during writing activities
- tricky or irregular words that will be useful
- subject-related – ie spelling the word 'conclusion' in science
- the pupil's own requests.

How many words?

The number of words in a list will vary according to the pupil. Better to set too few to begin with, you can always build on success; it is harder to back track from failure. Some pupils may only need one word on their list. Try asking the pupils; encourage them to improve on their own personal best.

Presenting the list

Make sure the list is written clearly and accurately to begin with. If pupils are copying down their own list, check it before they take it away. When learning a new pattern/sound, initially group together words with the same pattern/sound, eg stick, pick, trick. Then later contrast this sound with others, so the pupil has to make the distinction between them; stick, stink, pink, think, trick, pick.

Testing spelling

When testing the words that have been learned try the following tips:

● mix the words up, do not present them in the order of the list

● say each word clearly

● then say each word in its own sentence so that it is understood. This also helps with words that sound the same, eg sum, some (homophones).

● repeat the word on its own again and ask the pupil to write it

● test them again a few days later, a few weeks later, mix them up with other words, look out for them in a pupil's everyday writing – only then can you say if they have really have been learned

● can the pupils use the words to help with new ones, eg having learned 'table' can they use this knowledge to write 'stable'?

● can they write it in a sentence?

● keep accurate records of words that have been tested and the results, remember to date these – this will help you track progress, rate of learning and retention.

Classroom support

It is best to avoid over-reliance on dictionaries and word books, or on adults writing words for the pupil to copy. Guessing spellings based on letter sound knowledge and word patterns is important. This active approach will help improve independent spelling in the long term, as long as it is supported by careful teaching of letter sound correspondence. Giving a spelling without any requirement of a guess first, will only encourage a passive approach and an over-reliance on others. Always expect a preliminary guess before giving support, even if it is just the first letter. Respond with sensitive encouragement, perhaps ticking all the letters that were right and then showing which letters need to be changed.

What to do when asked for a spelling – simply VAK it!

● Can they 'stretch' the word as they say it and hear the sounds in sequence?

● If not, can they hear the sequence when you stretch the word?

● Can they write this down using their knowledge of letter sound correspondence?

● If not, have a letter sound chart that they can refer to.

● Does the word look right when they have written it?

● If they feel they can't write it all – Can they write the beginning or the end of it? You can add in the rest.

Encouraging guessing before asking

This can be done through:

● whiteboards and marker pens

● guessing paper (a sheet to be used just for guessing spellings)

● magic lines – where learners write the bits they know and put magic lines in for the rest

● linking to similar words/rimes already known, eg say – you know 'house' so how do you think you spell 'mouse'?

● spelling boxes drawn on paper for pupils to fill in. These are shaded to show the position of vowels and consonants.

Using dictionaries

Dictionaries should be encouraged as a checking device, not a first port of call. They should be used to *support* spelling and not take the place of it. Without some sort of initial guess, it is difficult to know where to begin a dictionary search.

The use of mini-whiteboards is ideal for this; a spelling error can easily be altered without making a mess of an original piece of work.

To avoid pupils aimlessly flicking through a dictionary, practise some of the following in your spelling sessions. These are all useful lifelong skills, as many adults who never did learn where individual letters come in order will testify. It is very useful to:

● know the 26 letter names and shapes – including different styles and fonts

● be able to order A-Z – with speedy recall – from any point

● have the immediate knowledge of individual letter positions within A-Z

● be able confidently to move backwards and forwards through the dictionary

● be able to scan down pages and columns for target letters and words

● use second and third letters, knowing that these are organised from A-Z, too

● use the guide words that are at the top of a dictionary page.

9: Developing social skills – particularly for pupils with SLCN and ASD

Stuart Norman

In the school environment, as in wider society, individuals are largely judged and defined by the quality of their interpersonal skills and social behaviour. The way they talk, act and present themselves to others; their recognition and understanding of emotional states in themselves and other people; the appropriateness of their verbal and non-verbal responses to others; their ability to instigate and successfully engage in social play; their capacity to cooperate with children and adults, to share and be flexible, are all barometers of their potential for social and educational inclusion.

While some pupils with speech, language and communication needs (SLCN) and autism spectrum disorders (ASD) may require local authority action and possibly statutory assessment, the social needs of many pupils in mainstream schools can be met through a differentiated curriculum and social skills intervention, perhaps through the avenues of School Action (SA) and School Action Plus (SAP). The most positive way of supporting pupils with communication difficulties is to take a whole-school team approach, with shared training and responsibilities, rather than just dealing with isolated or individual strategies. Where possible, this will include the input of other professionals, but there is still much the teacher and teaching assistant can do within the class and school setting to promote learning and social inclusion for pupils with a range of language impairments and communication needs.

The strategies outlined in this chapter have a proven record in effectively providing general and specific support for pupils with a range of communication difficulties – and also for pupils who have a statement of educational need for more severe and complex identified language and communication disorders, when placed in mainstream classes. An additional benefit is that many of the teaching and learning support mechanisms that are helpful for pupils with communication needs can be supportive for all pupils. Their success will depend on many factors, including consistency of approach and application, peer and parental support, and the willingness of the pupil to accept special interventions. However, many years' experience of placing these pupils in mainstream classes at Key Stage 2 has left no doubt in my mind that these strategies and approaches will lead to enhanced social and educational inclusion for many pupils who would otherwise be further distanced and isolated from their peers.

Using social stories

The social stories approach has been most clearly developed in America by Carol Gray (1994), in seeking to support pupils with autism or Asperger syndrome. It has since been taken up by many practitioners, as it is effective in enabling a pupil to understand and apply the cues and actions necessary for specific social situations. (Additionally it can also enable others to understand the perspective of pupils, and why their social behaviour can appear naïve, odd or disobedient.) In essence it is a strategy that involves writing a short 'story' to describe a target situation and the appropriate responses, actions and expressions. These in turn help pupils to respond or behave acceptably when next in that same situation. People with autism spectrum disorders and other communication difficulties have trouble reading the verbal and non-verbal behaviour of others, and are therefore unlikely to have access to accurate social information. They lack the ability to 'read' the thoughts or intentions of the other people in social contexts, often referred to as the 'theory of mind' deficit. This is compounded by the way in which they frequently focus on the details of a social encounter rather than the 'big picture'. If, for instance, such a pupil refers to a supply teacher or a fellow pupil as 'weird looking' or 'fat', he may cause embarrassment or hurt feelings in others, or even provoke anger, but none of these consequences are likely to be intended; they are simply a matter of literal, descriptive reference. Comments like these will often be understandably mistaken for disrespect, rudeness or non-compliance. Social stories aim to present pupils with direct access to social information with the minimum of potentially confusing instructional interaction.

Carole Gray suggests that basic social stories should contain three types of sentence:
● **Descriptive** sentences describe what happens, where a situation occurs, who is involved, what they are doing and why. They should be accurate, but include terms such as 'usually' or 'sometimes' rather than 'always'. This will help avoid literal interpretations, and also help allow for change.
● **Perspective** sentences describe the reactions and responses of others in target situations. They may also give the reasons for responses, and describe other peoples' feelings.
● **Directive** sentences describe desired responses to social situations, and tell the pupil in positive terms what she or he should try to do or say in the target situation. Inflexible statements should be avoided. 'I will try to' is preferable to 'I can' or 'I will' – either of which suggests absolute compliance to the literal pupil.

Gray suggests a ratio of at least three to five descriptive and perspective sentences for every directive sentence in a story, and warns against using too many directive sentences that may not leave room for a pupil to formulate a new response to a given situation.

Below is a single, but typical example of a successful social story which addressed a real situation in a Year 5 class. A pupil with SLCN had become increasingly anxious about attending a communication (TALK) group. As the pupil became aware it was near

TALK group time, he would invariably shout out to his teacher, asking what time it was, and if he should leave yet. This would continue, whatever his teacher was involved in, until he got a reply. Often it would become a socially disruptive element in the otherwise quietly productive classroom.

Waiting for TALK group

On Tuesdays TALK group time has changed to 2.30 in the afternoon.

I like going to TALK group and I like to get there on time.

Sometimes I think about getting to TALK group on time in my lesson before TALK group. I keep looking at the clock and asking my teacher about going to TALK group.

This means that I am not listening to the teacher and not concentrating on the lesson.

My teach is sad if I do this. I might not learn what I need to in class.

My teacher knows that I now go to TALK group at 2.30 and she will let me go in time.

I will try to concentrate on the lesson before TALK group. I will try not to look at the clock and not keep talking about when I am going to TALK group.

If I do, then I will be able to listen and learn in my lesson. My teacher will be happy.

She will tell me when to go to TALK group at the right time.

The story was written during a one-to-one session with a pupil by the adult who had obtained a full picture of the interactive factors involved, and, very importantly, the pupil's perspective. The story was shared with the other adults involved and a copy was also sent to parents. The story was to be formally read once a day. A copy in his tray could be referred to every time the pupil opened it in the classroom. However, this was hardly necessary as the results in this case were quite remarkable. There was an almost immediate change in the target behaviour. The social story was referred to by staff towards the end of the first day, but was completely unnecessary from the second day onwards. There were no further incidents of shouting out or anxieties about missing the TALK group; this pupil had added a new social skill to his repertoire, and had also developed greater social independence. More time has been given to social stories here as they, while not a magical 'cure-all' for all pupils with social communication difficulties, have a proven record of success. Although some training is necessary, or at least careful thought must be put into the writing of the social story according to the formula, the underlying strengths of social stories are apparent:

● they are visual, easily accessible and can be permanently available

● they are time efficient: once set up, they require comparatively little further adult input

● the results can be immediate

● they identify relevant social cues, and provide accurate information

● they provide scaffolding to help understand a social situation – they seek to teach meaning over rote compliance

● they are individualised and can be empowering for the pupil – pupils can have ownership over their own progress and learning.

Developing positive interactions: small group interventions

Teaching assistants (TAs) often have the task of supporting pupils who have pragmatic difficulties – difficulties that involve a poorly developed shared understanding of the rules and social use of language in any given context or environment. Developing these skills can be made more formalised and explicit for some pupils, in smaller groups, through the use of structured interventions such as Alison Schroeder's *Socially Speaking* (1996) or Wendy Rinaldi's *Social Use of Language Programme* (1992). These use specific games and activities to develop basic communication skills including:

● recognition of non-verbal body language and facial expressions

● emotional understanding

● friendship skills.

However, circle times can equally be used, often in a more inclusive way, to encourage appropriate social interaction and communication skills, within a whole-class setting. Circle time is now a central component of the social and emotional aspects of learning (SEAL) package being rolled out in schools at time of writing. There is also within SEAL a specific package for pupils with additional needs. This 'silver set' intervention is based on the principle that some children will benefit from exploring and extending their social, emotional and behavioural skills by being members of a supportive, small group that is facilitated by an empathic adult, such as a TA who has been part of whole-school training and familiarisation with the materials. This group should build on and enhance the curriculum being offered to each pupil within the whole-class setting. The class teacher should take overall responsibility for the group, including planning the curriculum being offered to each pupil and ensuring that it is consistent with whole-class activities. The teacher should work in partnership with the group-work TA who will explore key issues in more depth; facilitate personal development and risk taking; and practise new skills within a safe environment.

When leading any kind of group that includes pupils with SLCN and ASD needs it will be necessary to identify and teach four key components of what makes a good active listener, which will be central to all the other sessions:

● **Looking at the speaker** (while remembering that some pupils with communication difficulties, or who are on the autism spectrum, find it uncomfortable to look into other people's eyes – they can be encouraged to look at the mouth or in the general direction of the face of the speaker).

● **Sitting still** (also remembering that some pupils, who may be overactive or have coordination difficulties, can sometimes concentrate better if they have something to squeeze or hold – however, fidgeting may help focus, but it should not distract others).

● **Staying quiet** while the other person talks, and not talking themselves (and beginning to develop turn-taking skills).

● **Thinking** about what the speaker is saying (by being able to verbally communicate what has been said before, making a related comment of interest, or asking a relevant question).

These components can be displayed as permanent visual aids by using symbols or simple diagrams.

Raising awareness

Involving all pupils in the development of social skills has more benefits than working just with the targeted pupils. This approach reduces the risk that a learned dependency may be established through a constant pairing of the pupil with a teaching assistant. It also avoids singling out the pupil with the SLCN and ASD characteristics, which might introduce a further disadvantage before any interventions begin.

However, in some instances, highlighting pupil needs through sensitively developing peer (and adult) awareness in the school environment can have a major impact. If a pupil has particular social difficulties, for instance, with the physical proximity of others – ie, if they become anxious, upset or aggressive when other pupils 'invade' their personal space – this can be shared with the class, or with the whole school, if appropriate, in order to involve peers in reducing the likelihood of recurrence of the unwanted behaviour by helping to avoid the 'triggers' for that behaviour. Permission can be sought from the pupil and parents, and they can be asked if they wish to be present at a year group or whole-school assembly where the symptoms of a condition can be openly aired and demystified. This is particularly welcome if a pupil is aware of their own diagnosis of Asperger syndrome, for instance. Giving peers this kind of information can improve the frequency and quality of social interaction between the target pupil and classmates, and it can increase empathy towards the individual whose idiosyncrasies become more understandable and are not seen as intentionally provocative or awkward. In these circumstances, the TA can play a valuable role in articulating the specific needs of the pupil, and in the process, help to alleviate the problem.

Ideally there should also be a whole-school commitment towards the development of positive play and lunchtimes, with mentors, play leaders or lunchtime supervisors available to support socially vulnerable pupils. This approach could include a shared booklet which contains pen-portraits and photographs of pupils identified with particular characteristics such as lack of reciprocity, poor understanding of spoken language or inability to follow the shared rules of playground games. Again, teaching teams, in the information booklet, could provide simple guidelines describing supportive strategies for these pupils.

Using peer support

'Circles of friends' is an approach designed to work by prompting the young person's peers to identify social or behavioural difficulties, and to set targets and strategies themselves, with the long-term aim of increasing social integration and reducing anxiety. This problem-solving approach can be facilitated by a TA. The technique, based on original research in Canada, differs from circle time in that it takes a step-by-step approach to creating the circle of friends and is designed to help the classmates appreciate and empathise with a target pupil (as described, for instance, by Colin Newton and Derek Wilson in their book *Circle of Friends*, 1999). It runs over a set number of weeks and can be a powerful tool which, in seeking solutions from pupils in the 'front line', often steps outside of adult expectations or perceptions to bring about changes in surprising ways.

Less formally, it is valuable to encourage special 'buddies' and 'friendship circles' who can play with, and otherwise support, targeted pupils during breaks, clubs and less structured parts of the day. The aim is to help steer them away from inappropriate or conflict situations and to include them positively in both structured and unstructured games and activities. The selected peers can specifically model social skills, showing how to play and take turns, and by offering or seeking help if the child is teased. Again, a TA or other adult may be necessary to facilitate the group, recruit volunteers, set up rotas or manage disputes, when these are beyond the peer group's capabilities.

In class, it will be useful to make certain that all pupils have jobs or responsibilities to help build up self-esteem. Specific and structured activities can be shared with one or two selected classmates, who are more socially competent, to ensure the outcome is successful. This will be enhanced if the adults endeavour to foster a 'safe' classroom culture where it is OK to take risks, ask questions and get things wrong.

When working in groups, it will be necessary to check that there is a clear and worthwhile role for language-impaired pupils and to ensure they are meaningfully included, rather than sidelined by their peers. Many group techniques, such as 'jigsaw', 'snowballing' or 'reading detectives', will encourage this, where every member of the group will have a task that adds to or is essential to the desired outcome of an activity.

Using the physical environment

Many aspects of the school's physical environment could have a positive impact on the social skills and learning opportunities for a pupil with communication impairments.

- **Visual timetables** are particularly valuable. These can help orientate pupils throughout the school day, alert them to changes in routine activities, indicate duration of unstructured times, aid independence and minimalise reliance on teachers or assistants. Computer symbol software can be helpful here in standardising visual timetables across the school.
- **Standardised colour coding** can also be used to label drawers, equipment and other areas of the classroom, along with pictures and symbols to reduce frustrations or misunderstandings with peers.
- **Provide necessary equipment on the desktops** to minimise unnecessary disruptive movements around the classroom.
- If the class is sitting on the carpet, ensure the pupil is placed in a **prime listening position** to encourage attention. Fidgety or over-active pupils can often be 'anchored' to a spot by giving them their own 'carpet square' or marked position to sit on, in order to reduce unwanted physical interference of other pupils.
- Provide and distinguish between 'quiet areas' and 'discussion zones' in the classroom,

in order to cut down distracting background talk.

● Provide work stations for pupils who are easily distracted. These can be at windows where blinds are fitted!

Using visual prompts for understanding

Visual prompts and cues can reduce confusion and add to the independence and social inclusion of pupils with communication difficulties:

● Check on understanding and attention by requiring the pupil to identify the one or more key points from a teacher exposition. This can be by reporting back to a teacher or teaching assistant, by recording key information on a personal whiteboard or chart, or by checking against a visual prompt as below.

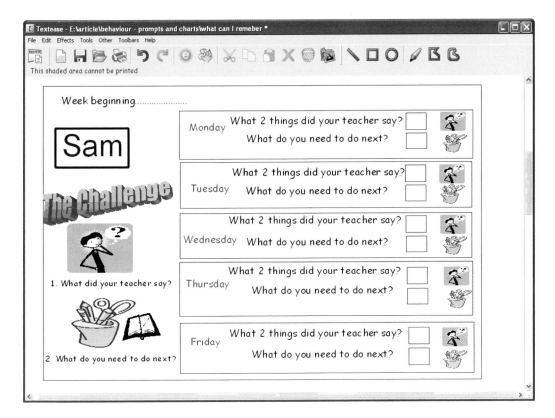

● Teach self-monitoring skills to increase ownership of the learning process. Pupils can be encouraged to identify when something is not understood (eg speaker is too loud or too quiet; competing noises; unfamiliar words; overlong or complex instructions), or there is a communication breakdown that will require clarifying questions. A signing system, or software which uses symbols can be used to help distinguish between how, what, why, when, which and where and other question words.

● Complex tasks can be broken into highly structured and shorter achievable steps to help allow independent work (multi-tasks can be visually listed in words and symbols on a personal whiteboard or pad, and ticked off as they are completed; a simple dot on the page can help to identify starting points and understand the desired length or extent of the work).

● Many pupils with language difficulties will be confused by the ambiguity of language, idioms and words with multiple meanings. They will frequently fail to appreciate irony, sarcasm and jokes based on wordplay. Such skills often need to be overtly taught using visual approaches. Use gesture and body language to reinforce spoken language. Where training is available, it is desirable to take on a signing system (such as Somerset Total Communication) as a whole-school strategy. Pupils find this easier to learn and use than most adults, and its use can further be encouraged if it is provided as an extra curricular club.

● Desirable social behaviours can be taught and reinforced using pictures, charts or photographs as below.

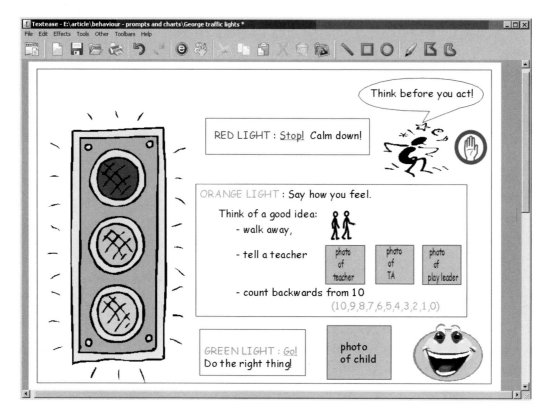

Graphic prompts that can be developed with and carried by the pupil at break times

Conclusion: Being proactive in developing effective collaboration

Finally, it is essential to support a consistent team approach and – ideally – be supported by a headteacher and SMT dedicated to giving SEN issues a high profile, and a staff with a can-do attitude to providing inclusive solutions to challenging needs. To meet these needs as a whole school it is necessary to provide dedicated collaboration, INSET and training time. However, TAs in mainstream schools are often the most significant figures for the pupil with SLCN and ASD needs, and a central point of contact for parents, and it is equally essential, therefore, for TAs to take a proactive approach in contributing to, and mediating, solution-focused interventions. TAs are central to the regular collaboration between all relevant parties to ensure additional social and learning needs are understood and meaningfully provided for throughout the school environment.

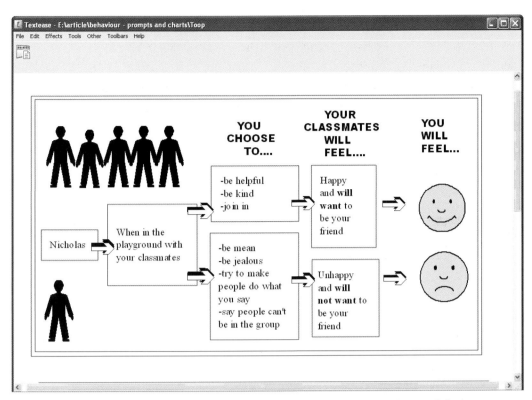

Reminders using the child's enthusiasms, interests and language abilities – following a circle time discussion with the target pupil's peers.

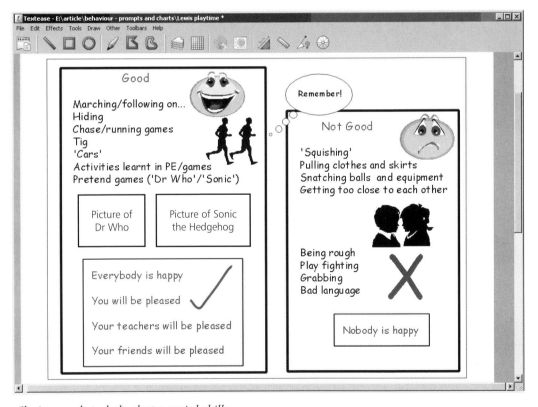

Choice cards to help shape social skills.

References

DfES (2005) *Social and Emotional Aspects of Learning – Improving Behaviour… Improving Learning.* London: DfES.

Gray, C (1994) *The New Social Story Book.* Arlington: Future Horizons.

Johnson, M. (1996) *Functional Language in the Classroom: A Handbook for Children with Communication Difficulties.* Manchester: Manchester Metropolitan University.

Newton, C and Wilson, D (1999) *Circle of Friends.* London: Folen.

Rinaldi, W (1992) *Social Use of Language Programme: Enhancing the Social Communication of Children and Teenagers with Special Needs.* Windsor: NFER- Nelson.

Schroeder, A (1996) *Socially Speaking: A Pragmatic Social Skills Programme for Pupils with Mild to Moderate Learning Disabilities.* Cambs: LDA.

10: Developing handwriting skills
Sue Soan

Pupils are now encouraged to use a word-processor from a very early age when producing 'best' work. For pupils with special educational needs, using a computer can support the development of comprehension and reading skills as well as self-esteem. However, without a doubt, there is still a need to provide every pupil with the skills and expertise to produce a clear, well formed handwritten script. Pupils' visual and spatial skills can be supported by developing their drawing and artistic techniques. Daily opportunities to practise fine motor skills, either through play, drawing or writing, are essential for a pupil to become a successful, confident writer.

In this chapter I am going to focus on how you as practitioners can really help pupils develop a well formed handwriting script. Many might think that this is quite a simple process, but just take a few minute to consider what skills young children especially require before they can write neatly and clearly.

For many pupils, a specific weekly handwriting lesson and daily writing tasks are enough to enable them to become satisfactory writers and suitably equipped to carry out other fine motor activities. However, for others the handwriting skills 'mastered' during a handwriting session cannot be transferred to any other school lesson. Some pupils in Years 4 and 5 may still only just be reaching the developmental stage (and some pupils with SEN will not even be there yet) when they are ready to produce a cursive script and are using fine motor skills requiring the expert manipulation of each individual digit. Efficient eye-hand coordination skills are also a vital element in developing any fine motor techniques. A simple activity can quickly inform you whether a pupil is developmentally advanced enough to carry out self-produced written tasks.

Ask the pupils you work with to touch their thumbs with each finger on the same hand; one at a time and one hand at a time. How many pupils find this difficult still, and do you consider this is the group of pupils who require additional or different fine motor activities? Of course, neither you nor teachers can produce individual programmes of support for handwriting skills, but there are a number of generic good practices, which, if part of the teacher's expectations, can positively enhance the opportunities for pupils to develop and practise these vital skills.

The following paragraphs illustrate a number of strategies that can be implemented into daily practice for everyone, but first it is important to ask yourself the following questions:

- Where are pupils expected to write and draw?
- How do pupils sit in the classroom when completely a written task?
- Is the furniture in the classroom/library/hall really suitable for encouraging good handwriting skills?
- Do you always ensure pupils are physically well prepared for the task to be completed?
- Is the equipment suitable?
- Is the lighting sufficient/without glare or reflection?

By answering such questions there are probably a couple of alterations you can make with the physical environment to help individual pupils without even having the need to think about curriculum changes or personalised plans.

Seating

Correct seating is very important; it is vital that tables and chairs are the right size, otherwise pupils will become quickly uncomfortable, causing fidgeting and also inappropriate seating position, let alone possibly causing back problems. I expect you have one or two pupils in your class you always appear to sit with one leg underneath them. Why do you think this might be? Observe when and why these pupils move into this position. How do you think your physical comfort effects your ability to focus and concentrate? If this is the case for adults, why do we expect anything different from pupils?

Hand-eye coordination

Pupils should, when writing:
- sit with both feet flat on the ground
- sit up straight with their back right against the back of the chair
- place their non-writing lower arm and hand horizontally along the desk edge, so that when they write their head and arms form a triangle.

These three important aspects help develop good hand-eye coordination and hence reading and spelling skills, as well as writing. They also support and strengthen a pupil's spine and provide the 'correct', most 'efficient' distance between the pupil's eyes and hand while writing. I find it surprising that in the majority of classrooms there is at least one pupil 'slouched' over his work. This is when the pupil uses his non-writing arm to support his head when writing. Undoubtedly this is to be discouraged, not only because the 'slouch' position means the pupil's spine gradually becomes weaker, but also because such a position means the hand-eye distance and direction is distorted, effecting the quality and quantity of the pupil's handwriting. Consequently this may also have detrimental effects on a pupil's reading, writing and spelling progress.

A teaching assistant should also recognise the need for a pupil to sit looking straight at a board or screen if he is being asked to copy or read from it. If this basic point is not considered and consistently acted upon, then those pupils with even slight visual memory difficulties or underdeveloped hand-eye coordination skills will find it very hard to copy, read or spell correctly. This is because the hand-eye system is hampered and interrupted, when a pupil with even the slightest of these problems has to turn to look at the board or screen and then turn back to the table to write it down. When turning, the pupil can so easily forget what letter he is writing and which line he is copying from, thus causing frustration and regular risks of failure. Consequently, the seating position of every pupil in a class needs extremely careful thought.

To help instil this 'good sitting' regime, introduce the pupils to a rhyme you can all practice, together at the start of the lesson or they can 'sing' internally on their own when necessary. Try the following words to the rhythm of 'One, two, buckle my shoe':

One, two feet on the floor
Three, four sit up quite straight
Five, six pick up your pen
Seven, eight steady your arm
Nine, ten ready to write.

Left-handed writers

So many instances in these modern times still necessitate pupils who use their left-hand to carry out fine motor tasks to find strategies to cope in a right-handed orientated environment. However, with correct advice and instruction during early schooling, many problems for left-handed writers, in particular, can be avoided. First, following on from the issues mentioned above always remember to seat a pupil who is a left-handed writer on the left-hand side of a right-handed pupil. You will be surprised how many disagreements and shouts of 'he's pushing me!' can be so quickly and easily prevented, let alone by the decline of spilt drinks and paint pots!'

Good practice indicates that left-handed writers should be encouraged to have their books and sheets of writing paper tilted at about a 45 degree angle to the left at all times. If this is not actively and consistently modelled and supported during the primary school years, difficulties may develop such as:

- a 'hook' pencil grip
- general poor handwriting
- smudging of work (if using ink/fluid)
- poor visual memory leading to comprehension, reading and spelling problems.

The reasons for this are quite straightforward. If a left-handed pupil is expected to write on a page positioned straight in front of him, he cannot see what he is writing or has just written. In this circumstance, a pupil will most probably begin to raise his writing hand above the page into a 'hook' position to be able to see his work. If a flat hand is used, the pupil may well ruin his work as he goes, if he uses ink, smudging everything. Also, most significantly, by covering the word he has just written, a pupil's continuity of thought and understanding can be easily broken, hindering the development of spelling and reading skills. If you have not seen this, watch a left-handed writer to see what strategies they have developed to cope in similar situations. However, this simple slanting of a page can effectively solve all the issues mentioned if introduced at an early stage in a supportive and positive manner.

The tripod grip

This is the grip which supports the most efficient and effective method of handwriting. With an incorrect pen/pencil grip a pupil can very quickly experience physical problems, such as hands/arms arching and tiredness. Other issues arising from an incorrect grip may be:

● poor pressure, either heavy or light, on the pencil, leading to handwriting difficulties

● poorly formed letters and numbers

● poor, immature grip.

The grip needs to be modelled by the practitioners in the classroom; practiced and encouraged for all pupils as is illustrated below (see Figure 1). For those pupils who find the tripod grip difficult, triangular pencils, crayons and pens can be purchased from a variety of suppliers (see Resources). These encourage the 'correct' grip and support the pupil in gaining a flowing and clear handwriting. Not surprisingly it is also important for the pupils to hold their pencil or pen in the most appropriate place. The pupil's finger tips should be placed at the end of the coloured section of a pencil and just above the nib of a pen. This ensures that the pupil can still see the tip of the pencil lead or nib, while maintaining a well supported position. Additionally, the pencil or pen should rest comfortably in the recess between the thumb and the index finger. This is vital because, by doing this, the pencil's 'good' position will be maintained without the need for the pupil to grip the pencil too tightly, preparing aches and tiredness.

Figure 1: tripod grip

Work surfaces and sloping boards

For developing all hand-eye skills, but especially handwriting, a sloping surface can be very beneficial. Why? A sloping surface encourages:

● the correct seating position

● the pupil's ability to 'feel' how much pressure should be placed on the pencil

● good hand-eye skills, especially when pupils are required to copy from a classroom screen or board, and reading of course.

Individual sloping boards can be purchased, or for older pupils, even A4 ring binders placed on their sides can be extremely helpful. I have also found that a sloping board can be very useful in creating a working boundary for pupils. This can be most effective for pupils with autism, Asperger syndrome, dyspraxia or memory organisational difficulties. In this way, a pupil with autism, for example, knows where exactly his boundary is, as do his neighbours. Also, a pupil can store his equipment either on the sloping board or under it, meaning that there are fewer opportunities for pencils, rulers etc, to be moved or touched, even accidentally.

It is only now that all these other issues have been considered that the actual process of teaching letter formation and the skills of handwriting should be commenced.

Handwriting skills

There are many different commercial schemes that a school can use as a basic guide. The development of a joined cursive script is the aim for every pupil. It is vital, however, that pupils really can 'feel' and visualise the movement and shape of letters, and although this is mostly only supported in early years' classrooms, it is important for older children with motor skills needs still to have these opportunities offered to them. Examples of good practice in the classroom for encouraging correct letter formation include:

● writing letter shapes in the air

● forming letters in sand, or even more successful is the forming of letters in icing sugar!

● tracing over wooden or brightly coloured foam or plastic letters

● dot-to-dot pictures and letters

● tracing over shapes, starting and ending without a break at the correct places

● tracing the formation of a letter on the back of a peer and then asking them which letter it is

● forming a letter on paper with a blindfold on really makes pupils think about shape, size and positioning.

The use of 'entry' and 'exit' links (see Figure 2, below) enables pupils to maintain a flow to their writing and encourages the 'joining' of letters nearly immediately. Young writers particularly should not be expected to produce a really tidy, even script to begin with, but with good teaching this will improve quite quickly for the majority of pupils. This method of using a cursive script is particularly beneficial for pupils with dyslexia or other visual memory issues, because forming a whole work without taking the pencil off of the page, supports the spelling, reading and visualisation of a word.

Finally, it is important to recognise that handwriting is not just about putting a pencil to paper. The physical environment, tools and physical wellbeing of the pupils are also vital aspects of developing good handwriting skills. The difficulty of achieving a coherent, well formed and even script can be seen around us every day – just observe the writing of colleagues, family members and friends, noting how they sit, hold their writing equipment and position their paper. You will now probably be able to identify why their writing is not clear, even or well formed. By ensuring the basic skills are in place, you enable pupils to become clear, efficient and effective writers.

Have a go!

Figure 2: Entry and exit links

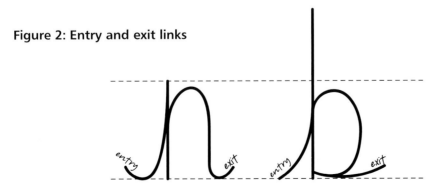

Resources

ACE Centre Advisory Trust, Waynflete Road, Headington, Oxford OX3 8DD. Tel: 01865 63508 www.ace-centre.org.uk go to 'Resources'

Advance Seating Designs, Unit 7, Everitt Road, London NW10 6PL. Tel: 0181 961 4515 www.asd.co.uk

Berol Ltd, Oldmeadow Road, Kings Lynn, Norfolk PE30 4JR. Tel: 01553 761221 www.berol.co.uk

CALL Centre, University of Edinburgh, 4 Buccleugh Place, Edinburgh EH8 9LW. Tel:01316671438 http://callcentre.education.ed.ac.uk/Resources/resources.html

Hope Education, Orb Mill, Culvert Street, Oldham, Lancashire OL4 2ST. Tel: 0161 633 6611

Homecraft Supplies Ltd, Sidings Road, Low Moor Estate, Kirkby in Ashfield, Notts NG177JZ. Tel: 01623 754047 http://information.downsed.org/library/books/meeting-ed-needs/ed-needs-appendix1-EN-GB.htm

LDA – www.ldalearning.com/scripts/searchcat.php

Philip & Tacey, Northway, Andover, Hampshire SP10 5BA. Tel: 01264 332171 www.philipandtacey.co.uk

Special Needs Kids – www.special-needs-kids.co.uk/toys-motorskills.htm

11: Working with pupils with a speech, language and communication need

Mary Hartshorne

What are speech and language difficulties?

It is expected that when pupils start school they are competent communicators: able to listen to and understand long instructions, speak clearly in complete sentences, have conversations – maybe making an occasional mistake. For many pupils this is not the case; an increasing number start school with immature language. As well as this, as many as one in 10 pupils have a speech, language or communication difficulty (SLCD). This means that it is likely that there will be several pupils in every primary classroom who may have difficulty paying attention, understanding, expressing themselves or using language to make friends and socialise.

Confusingly, there are many different terms used to describe speech and language difficulties. You might hear communication disability, language disorder, specific language impairment. All of these terms mean that pupils may have problems in the following areas:

● **Processing** lots of spoken language (listening, making sense of what they have heard, formulating a response).

● **Understanding** instructions, words, ideas.

● **Expressing** themselves (using clear speech in complete sentences).

● **Using** language socially to interact with other pupils and adults.

Pupils can have difficulty with just one of these aspects, or with a combination, depending on how complex their difficulties are.

Why are speech and language skills so important?

Communication skills are essential for all different aspects of school: learning, socialising and behaving. Pupils need good speech and language skills to learn to read and then go on to do well academically, feeling good about themselves. Playing, making friends, solving problems and learning new words and ideas are all dependent on a solid foundation of good speech and language skills. As well as this, pupils need speech and language skills to help keep calm and understand and regulate their emotions and feelings. We know from studies that pupils with speech and language difficulties are more at risk of literacy difficulties, poorer academic achievement and low self-esteem, and they are more likely to find friendships difficult. There is also a strong relationship between speech and language difficulties and emotional and behavioural problems.

What can be done to support language development at school?

Pupils learn to talk by interacting with more confident speakers: both adults and pupils. The more opportunity pupils get to talk, the better they will get at speaking and listening. Sometimes they will need adults to structure and support interaction – the type of support we give them is really important. Very often, adults feel that they have to get pupils to do language activities, games, worksheets. What is more powerful, is thinking about what we as adults do, how we interact with pupils, and how we structure our classrooms so they are 'communication-friendly environments'.

How can teaching assistants help?

Teaching assistants (TA) have a key role to play in creating a communication-friendly environment. You are often the people who have time/are able to develop good relationships with pupils, who have more opportunity to talk in small groups or on a one-to-one basis.

Often it can be difficult to know whether you are doing the right thing.

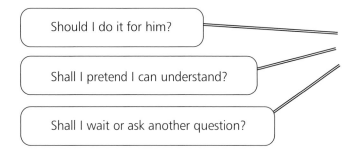

This chapter will give you some handy hints for supporting pupils' communication. If you are worried about a pupil's communication, it is important to talk through your concerns with the class teacher or school SENCO. There may already be other people involved who can give you advice related more specifically to the pupil.

Thinking about talking

It is worth taking a few minutes to think about a pupil's speech and language. This doesn't need to take a long time, but it might give you a chance to reflect on how they are communicating. It can often be helpful to think about when a pupil seems most comfortable chatting, and when they have most difficulties. Complete the following short questionnaire; it might give you some surprises.

And now your turn, how are *you* talking with pupils? When you are with the pupils you work with, who does most of the talking? What type of language do you use? Reflecting on your own style can be really helpful – however quickly you do it. Taping or videoing is best, but getting someone to observe you is fine. Even if you make an effort to actively think about what you are doing, this will give you a bit of feedback. Adults who have done this have often been surprised: 'I never stop talking, no wonder they don't talk, they can't get a word in!', 'I didn't realise I asked so many questions', 'I interrupted him, didn't I?' 'I say "super" all the time, don't I?!'.

Talking checklist

Name:

Date:

Comments:

Who do they choose to talk with most?

When do they talk most?
- ☐ in class
- ☐ group work
- ☐ pair work
- ☐ practical activities
- ☐ play activities
- ☐ in the playground
- ☐ when it's just one person

What do they like talking about?

Example of longest sentence:

What do they do when they don't understand?
- ☐ ask a question
- ☐ go quiet
- ☐ get annoyed
- ☐ hit out
- ☐ _____

How do they communicate?
- ☐ talking
- ☐ pointing/looking
- ☐ gesture/facial expression
- ☐ physically showing/pulling
- ☐ _____

Use a simple checklist to reflect on your own communication style – you don't need to share it with anyone!

Handy hints – general

The following tips and strategies will help you to support all pupils' language development.

Understanding comes before expression

It is tempting to focus solely on encouraging pupils to talk, to say longer sentences and new words. Even if a pupil is not chatting away, they can be developing their language through activities such as listening to longer instructions, sorting new words, joining in games. Keep the pressure off by not expecting too much chatter.

Your talking

Listen to yourself, get someone to observe, or tape yourself when you are talking with a child or small group – just for a few minutes.

How many times do you talk?

How many times do the children talk?

How many questions do you ask?

What kind of question?
- [ ] closed (one-word answers)
- [ ] open

How long do you wait for children to reply?

Notice your non-verbal communication:
- [ ] are you at their level?
- [ ] do you use your hands?
- [ ] facial expression?

Any other comments?

Wait, allow thinking time

This is one of the hardest things to do, it is so tempting to fill in all the gaps to keep a conversation going. Remember, pupils need time to process information. They will often come up with an answer or response if you give them time to think. Encourage the process by saying you're giving them 'thinking time', or by using 'encouragers' such as 'uh huh', 'really' etc.

Praise for speaking and listening

Often we give praise for good work, or a good achievement – but we miss out on acknowledging good speaking, listening or interacting. We frequently point out when things are wrong, but not when interaction is successful. Pupils need positive as well as negative feedback.

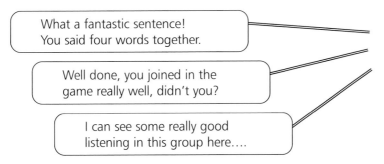

> What a fantastic sentence! You said four words together.

> Well done, you joined in the game really well, didn't you?

> I can see some really good listening in this group here....

Use words to talk about language

We can raise pupils' awareness of their language skills by using language such as 'word', 'sentence', 'conversation', 'sounds' when we are giving feedback to them. This gives them an accurate picture of how they are as a communicator. We call this developing their 'metalinguistic' skills – their awareness of language.

Give extra visual information

Pupils with language difficulties often find information presented visually easier to understand and follow. Think creatively about how you can supplement your spoken language with non-verbal information. This can be with a gesture, a facial expression, through demonstration – showing as well as telling, picture, objects. One of the most effective ways to create a communication-friendly environment is through the use of visual timetables: a sequence of photographs, symbols or pictures which represent a

---

Encouraging talking

Use a range of ways to start conversations.
Every child is different.

Closed question
Example: Did you have a good time at the zoo?

Open question
Example: What was it like at the zoo?

Encouraging talking continued

Tell me...
Example: Tell me about your trip to the zoo.

Alternatives
Example: Did you see elephants or lions at the zoo?

Comment
Example: I was just thinking about your day at the zoo...
I went to the zoo last week...
Zoos are really exciting aren't they...?

Commentary
Example: Let's draw a picture of the zoo, I wonder what we should put in.
I'm thinking about the animals we saw...
oh and you're drawing the lion, with a... oh it's a lion cub.
I'll draw the next cage, now I'm trying to remember what... that's right the bears, with...

---

routine or series of events. More information and examples of visual timetables can be found at www.talkingpoint.org.uk

Talk Time

Speaking and listening 'rules'

All children need to know how to speak and listen. Many classrooms now have posters of active speaking and listening skills up on the wall. These might be 'sit still', 'one person talks at a time', 'give each other time to talk', 'look at the person speaking', 'say when you don't understand'. It is important that children know these are for adults in the classroom as well! If these posters are used as reminders of 'good speaking' and 'good listening' then you can target praise more easily.

Create opportunities

Children who are reluctant to talk often need a reason to communicate. When there is lots to get through, it is very easy to focus on doing and not talking – some children go through the whole day without the need to talk. Try and create opportunities for children to talk: think of messages that need to be sent (you can make them simple or complicated), make deliberate or funny mistakes, leave out an essential piece of equipment so they have to ask for something, play the fool 'Now then, what do we need here...?', 'I'm a bit confused...'

A lovely way to encourage communication between school and families is to stick something in a home/school book that represents what has gone on during the day (a leaf, wrapper from a food, sticker, ticket) so that parents/carers can ask about it. This works really well the other way round, and gives you information about what children have been up to at home.

Handy hints – expression

The following tips and strategies will help you to support pupils who have difficulty producing spoken language/getting their message across.

Don't pretend you understand

It is sometimes hard to know how to respond when you really can't tell what a pupil is saying. Don't panic, let them know that it's OK and you'll try and work it out together:

● ask them to say it again

● apologise – 'sorry, I didn't hear'

● give them other strategies – 'can you use another word?'/'can you show me?'/'can you draw me a picture'

● if all fails, don't pretend you have understood if you haven't – apologise and move on: 'Sorry, I can't understand that word, tell me about X instead.'

If a pupil's speech is very difficult to understand, try to keep the context known to both of you – talk about something you've done together or both know about to narrow down what it is the pupil might be talking about.

Extend their sentences

There are different ways to support pupils in developing longer sentences through the feedback you give them. We can recast, rephrase or expand.

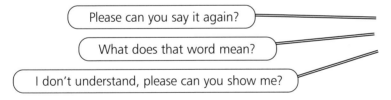

We can ask questions if we don't understand

- Please can you say it again?
- What does that word mean?
- I don't understand, please can you show me?

Signpost

For longer stretches of spoken language such as stories, explanations or reporting back in class, you can support pupils by giving them spoken prompts which will help to structure their stories such as 'first', 'and then', 'so' and 'next'.

Questions, questions

Lots of people find that when they listen to themselves, they are surprised at how many questions they ask – and often these are 'closed questions'. Closed questions only need a one word response, often 'yes' or 'no'. Questions can sometimes stop a child talking, not encourage them. Think about starting a conversation with a comment, with 'tell me about...' or using an open question. Some children may need some alternatives to get them started. Often questions can put too much pressure on children and it can be better to talk alongside children while you are doing an activity rather like a commentary, or verbalising your thoughts. Remember to leave lots of pauses for them to join in.

Vocabulary games

In all of these games, use pictures, words or real objects but make sure you say the words as often as possible

- **Pairs** – pairs of pictures, cards face down. Take turns to turn over two cards and find matching pairs.
- **Bingo** – adult or child takes card out of a bag and give a definition, child matches to the right picture.
- **Connections** – make a chain of cards across the table. You can only joint card on to the line if you can think of how it 'goes with' the one next to it. Meaning or sound reasons accepted!
- **Attribute!** – pass an object around a group, each child has to say something about it when they hold it. Winner is the person left at the end.
- **Feely bag** – real objects in a bag, put you hand in and guess what you feel.
- **Ranking** – order cards top to bottom between criteria, could be 'biggest/smallest', 'loudest/quietest', 'nice to eat/horrid to eat' – whatever fits!
- **Four corners** – have a word in each corner of the room, children run to the one you describe; sometimes there could be two possible corners - leads to discussion.
- **Post box** – sort pictures into categories, have different boxes for different groups 'round things', 'things you eat', 'animals' – whatever fits!
- **Guess what?** – adult or child hides a picture, others ask questions to find out what it is OR clues are given so the rest can guess what it is.
- **Syllable bingo** – children have bingo cards with numbers between 1 and 4. Adult or child pull out a card out of a pile/bag and names it. You call if you have the right number of syllables.

Handy hints – understanding

The following tips and strategies will help you to support pupils who have difficulty understanding spoken language:

- slow down
- emphasise key words
- encourage questions
- think about the vocabulary you use.

Handy hints – social interaction

To help children with communication problems interact with other people:

- script social situations
- provide a commentary
- model successful interaction
- provide structure.

Resources

Anne Locke's *Living Language* www.onestopeducation.co.uk/icat/40180

Talking point www.talkingpoint.org.uk

Black Sheep Press www.blacksheep-epress.com/system/index.html

Index

Index